#1

I0440274

In My Computer

Miltos Manetas

LINK EDITIONS

LINK Editions

Domenico Quaranta, *In Your Computer*, 2011

Valentina Tanni, *Random*, 2011

Miltos Manetas, *In My Computer – Miltos Manetas*, 2011

Miltos Manetas
In My Computer

Publisher: LINK Editions, Brescia, May 2011
www.linkartcenter.eu

Printed and distributed by: Lulu.com
www.lulu.com

ISBN 978-1-4477-1939-7

«I actually know for sure that there are scenes on the Internet that nobody knows about and nobody cares about, and within those milieus, very specialized sensibilities are evolving.»

_ William Gibson, 2003

From *Wikipedia, the Free Encyclopedia* (link visited on May 17, 2011):

Miltos Manetas (born October 6, 1964 in Athens) is a Greek painter and multimedia artist. He currently lives and works in Highgate. Manetas has created Internet Art as well as paintings of cables, computers, video games and Internet websites. His work has been collected by Charles Saatchi. He is also the founder of "Neen", an Internet-based art movement. Manetas presented the Whitneybiennial.com, an online exhibition that challenged the 2002 Whitney Biennial show.

Googlism for: miltos manetas:

miltos manetas is the net
miltos manetas is best known in
miltos manetas is lying on a brown psychoanalyst's couch that constitutes the only colorful furniture in the entire white and gray loft that he inhabits with
miltos manetas is an artist
miltos manetas is similar
miltos manetas is known for his paintings of computer hardware and vibracolor prints
miltos manetas is one of the artists who addresses these mixed messages
miltos manetas is a greek artist who works and lives between los angeles and new york city
miltos manetas is not an evil force magdalena sawon
miltos manetas is a ny/la
miltos manetas is an artist whose paintings mostly explore the realm of computers

Contents

Editor's Note

This book is the result of a productive process that would have been impossible just ten years ago. I'm not talking only about "material" things such as productive structures and distribution infrastructures, but also about immaterial things such as speed, working conditions, and the way ideas take shape and circulate.

Some months ago, I decided to make a test with print-on-demand (POD). I collected some things I wrote in the past, I edited them, I wrote an introduction and I made a book, *In Your Computer*. In the meantime, I was working hard with some partners in crime to set up an institution, the LINK Center for the Arts of the Information Age. Publishing books was part of our mission, and the POD approach had much in common with our vision: accessibility of tools, free circulation of knowledge, international audience. So, we decided to make the book together, and to conceive it as the first outcome of an ongoing editorial effort.

In Your Computer was released on May 5, 2011. At the time, I still didn't know what would have happened in the following weeks. What I knew was that, in less than a month, another beautiful dream was going to turn real. It wasn't my dream, but Miltos Manetas, who had it, was cool enough to share it with me and many other people.

This dream is called "The Internet Pavilion", but the name may be misleading. The Internet Pavilion is not the nth boring pavilion of a messy art event. It is an informal gathering of like-minded people, a temporary autonomous zone, an island in the net, a place where to exchange, copy and share beautiful ideas.

We wanted to share our beautiful idea with other people. We had the place. But one book was not enough to show how beautiful it was. We needed at least three books. We had to make them in a month, and tell people about it.

Random, the second book, was the result of a Sunday morning conversation between Fabio Paris, one of my partners in crime, and Valentina Tanni. *Random* – the online magazine Valentina launched in 2001 – was approaching its tenth birthday, and she wanted to do something to celebrate it. «Why not a book?», Fabio said. The day after, I e-mailed Valentina the bad news: the book should be ready in 23 days.

The next e-mail was for Miltos. Miltos is not just the beloved father of the Internet Pavilion. He is also the author of some seminal texts which had a long lasting influence on me and many other people. He is a great artist. He has been one of the earlier experimenters of POD (*100 Years After Les Demoiselles D'Avignon*, published with Cafe Press, dates back to 2007). Finally, with the "Piracy Manifesto" and many other earlier texts, he helped shaping the mind-frame you need in order to understand what we are doing with LINK Editions. I had to persuade him.

What follows can be read as a Gospel parable – a literary genre that Miltos seems to like a lot. We arranged a meeting in Milan. I went to him with a book in my hands, and an idea in my mind. In about ten minutes, he took the book, took the idea, remixed them and came out with an unexpected, brand new thing. «I like the title of your book, can I borrow it?» «Sure.» «You'd better use it for all the books you are going to publish. You ask authors to collect and share spare fragments of text available on their computer, and you publish them all with the same title, *In Your Computer* – the only difference being the author's name and the book's contents.»

I loved the idea. I took it and I brought it with me in the underground. Then, I phoned Fabio. Discussing with him, the idea changed shape again.

The book you hold in your hands, or you read on your screen, is the result of this fast, invisible process. Ideas moving from mind to mind, circulating freely on phone lines and internet connections, and being reshaped and refined at every step. Who does it belong to? To hackers, who first said «we love your computer»? To Jodi, who turned this sentence into «we are honored to be in somebody's computer»? To me, who fourteen years later decided to call my book *In Your Computer*? To Miltos, who wanted to steal my title? To Fabio, who rephrased it into *In My Computer*?

The truth is that this idea doesn't belong to any of us. It belongs to You, my beloved reader. Take it, reshape it, turn it into something better, and set it free again. This is one of the wonderful messages that Miltos is delivering to You, and to his upcoming daughter, with this book. Here, he collected some texts already available online, not necessarily in the present form, and a selection of private writings, email exchanges, notes taken on a Smartphone. This is his personal time box, and it's open source. I hope you will enjoy its contents as I did.

Domenico Quaranta, Brescia, May 21, 2011

Introduction

Contemporary Art artists, are not the only active artists around. There are still Surrealists in Paris, Abstract Expressionists in NY, even Impressionists who still paint flowers and mountains in their pathetic studios in Amsterdam and Rome.

All these people have their magazines, their galleries and their critics. Societies don't disappear easily because people tend to defend their style and their way of life. The Surrealists still give a lot of importance to their imagination, the Expressionists still drink a lot etc. They all try their best and most of them are very charismatic people, but Art – which is a Dancing Queen – in Life's nightclub gets bored after a while, and then she moves to another table. When she abandons a group of people she takes her gifts back. Radicalism, the spirit of invention, pretty girls and young boys, they are all gone. What's left is only fatigue.

For last, she takes away the specter of power and authority and gives it to some new people which nobody had noticed until then.

Today (2011), one hundred and four years after *Les Demoiselles d'Avignon*, it's time for changes again. Europe, Asia and America, are still dominated by Conceptual artists. There are all the flavors: Minimalists, Installators, Social agit props, Old Neogeos, Documenta fighters, Flash Art Coverpagers. All these people are in rotation around the concept of the Real Space. They seldom have the time to play with videogames because they are busy with walls to touch, rooms to fill and objects to invent. A big photo in a frame. A small photo, unframed in an empty room. A video played on a TV or a video projection. New British Art. An old object in a new combination, a composition of elements from the language of this artist, some paintings, a text – more important as an image than an image – and some over scaled dolls and colorful toys with metaphorical power and many things in boxes so they look German and serious.

The clan of these people seems to be the right one: It is powerful and exclusive, full with cool young people. It's the clan of Contemporary Art. In the same way that there are still Surrealists, Abstract Expressionists and Impressionists, there are many Contemporary Art artists.

And then, somewhere, there must exist some NewPeople and these are the people that I am curious about.

Miltos Manetas, Rome 2011

This text has been written by Miltos Manetas in New York in 1997, and circulated with the title "NewPeople". We republish it here unchanged, except for the dates and the title.

Playstation Time. Art, Games and Video

Miltos Manetas speaks with Lionel Bovier, Christophe Cherix & John Tremblay in Brooklyn, NY, on the 6th of April 199□.

At the end of a very normal day, Miltos Manetas is lying on a brown psychoanalyst's couch that constitutes the only colorful furniture in the entire white and gray loft that he inhabits with Vanessa Beecroft. He has positioned three seats next to it, albeit placing himself in the situation of an analyzed. The conversation below is the exact transcription of this lacanian "floating listening" session...

LIONEL BOVIER: YESTERDAY, WE WERE WATCHING YOUR NEW VIDEOS AND DISCUSSING THE PRECISE NATURE OF THE GAP EXISTING BETWEEN THEM AND THEIR REFERENT (IE. SOME SPECIFIC AND ACTUAL VIDEOGAMES) HOW COULD YOU DEFINE YOUR RELATIONSHIP TO VIDEO?

My relationship with video is conflictual. From one side, I suppose that I have to make a few videos because it's a medium easy to handle – it's convenient and cheap – but from the other side, I hate video. In a way, it's even worse than cinema: you have to watch it in a box, framing the images. So if I had to make a real video film, I would have to work hard for something that doesn't represent me entirely... So when I bought my Sony PlayStation I discovered a fast way to make videos: I just have to record a part of a game that linked to something I'm interested in showing or expressing. The images are coming from a precedent scenario that I can use and are appropriated just by playing the game...

For example; for the video series *Flames* (1997) which I made from the game Tomb Raider, I had the girl (Lara Croft) run into a cave with arrows coming from all around. She got hit with them until she fell dead on the snow, mourning a moving "ah". I had her run, repeatedly into a tape for ten minutes. Ten times she tried to cross the corridor, but she always faltered and died. It fulfilled my wishes for a story about weakness, beauty, and tragedy. It was as if it was designed for me, waiting for me in the stores to buy it and use it. Moreover, it's technically made exactly like a real video because in the game you can decide how to move the girl, from which point of view you want to film her, etc... So you are actually the real director of the game session. The only difference is that the actor is virtual and the sets, stage lighting, and so on, are ready-made from the game's programmer. A second video is made from a flight simulator in which you are supposed to fly an airplane in the sky, but it runs endlessly on the water. The video is called *Miracle 1996*, in memory of the famous Jesus miracle. I like Jesus miracles, which as Gerald Lynn said are very credible because they include such astonishing details, that you end up believing them. Once, in a wedding (not a proper occasion for a miracle), Jesus transformed a whole river into wine...

JOHN TREMBLAY: I JUST PERFORMED A MIRACLE: I TRANSFORMED REGULAR BREAD INTO TOAST! IF SOMEBODY NEEDS SOME...

LIONEL BOVIER: I UNDERSTAND THAT YOU ARE USING AN ERROR IN THE PROGRAMMING OF THE GAME TO HAVE YOUR WORK DONE, IS THAT RIGHT? SOME KIND OF FREE SPACE IN THE PRECONCEIVED SCENARIOS...

Yes, I like mistakes, bugs, and failure of computer's functions as much as their abilities and performances. *Miracle 1996* is an experience of the limits of a game situation and the sudden implosion of every competence.

The main subject that I choose to represent with my work is the moment when ability fades. It's a classical topic. You can find it, for instance, in the book by Heinrich Von Kleist, *The Prince of Homburg*. In the story, a young prince falls asleep and forgets the battle he was supposed to join.

LIONEL BOVIER: DO YOU REALLY ALWAYS NEED TO ORGANIZE YOUR WORK ON SUCH SPECIFIC THEMES?

I need a subject. I don't believe in abstract art. I think I am always relating to representation.

LIONEL BOVIER: THAT REMINDS ME OF THE COLLECTION OF CHARACTERS THAT YOU STARTED IN 1993 (AND CALLED, AS IN THE "FIGURATION" SIDE OF CINEMA'S JOBS, EXTRAS).

JOHN TREMBLAY: WHAT?

LIONEL BOVIER: MILTOS COLLECTED IN HIS COMPUTER HUNDREDS OF DESCRIPTIONS OF FICTIONAL CHARACTERS AND JUST EDITED THE LIST. YOU HAVE TO READ THAT

"BOOK," IT'S EXCITING AND AT THE SAME TIME REACHING A POINT OF PERFECT VOID.

JOHN TREMBLAY: IS IT INFINITE?

Yes, it's a never-ending process. I go to libraries and copy in my Powerbook the descriptions. What I wanted to do was to create a book from the material which I usually avoid reading.

JOHN TREMBLAY: WHY DON'T YOU READ THESE TYPE OF DESCRIPTIONS NORMALLY?

Because my focus in literature, as in life, consists in the generic and not in the individual or the particular, I try to avoid looking at the features or the details of things. I want to see the whole image – or the image as a whole. This attitude is then pushed to the opposite. I make art just to be able to make the opposite of what I really should do. I even became a painter recently... because I never had any interest in painting something...

JOHN TREMBLAY: HERE, I'VE ONE DESCRIPTION FROM BORIS VIAN TO ADD TO YOUR COLLECTION: «HE WAS REASONABLY TALL AND SLIM-HIPPED; HE HAD LONG LEGS AND WAS VERY, VERY NICE. THE NAME COLIN SUITED HIM ALMOST PERFECTLY. HE TALKED TO GIRLS WITH CHARM AND TO BOYS WITH PLEASURE. HE WAS ALWAYS IN A GOOD MOOD AND THE REST OF THE TIME HE SLEPT.»

CHRISTOPHE CHERIX: I PLAYED THE GAME [TOMB RAIDER] YESTERDAY AND FOUND VERY PERVERSE THAT YOU CONTINUOUSLY KILLED THE GIRL IN YOUR VIDEO. THE DEATH YOU ARE SHOWING IS IN FACT THE ONE OF YOUR OWN IDENTIFICATION WITH THE GAME. I WOULDN'T CALL IT A FAILURE, BECAUSE THIS IS INSCRIBED IN THE MAIN PURPOSES OF THE GAME. LOOK AT THE DELICATE WAY IN WHICH THE CHARACTER IS DYING! WHAT I WOULD LIKE TO KNOW IS WHY YOU CHOOSE THESE SPECIFIC SETS (IN A CAVE, WITH ARROWS OR DIFFERENT CUTTING OBJECTS) AND NOT OTHERS. AND HOW WOULD YOU INTERPRET THE SUICIDAL WAY YOU PURPOSELY PLAYED?

First, I like that confusion of identity. As a player, you are the girl character, but you are also the director of the video in which she is (or you are) acting. Then I choose specific sets that underline what I wanted to express. Moreover, when the character dies it is impossible for you to see the rest of the landscapes in the game, which are actually very beautiful.

With her death, understanding becomes impossible because what in real life is movement and motion, in the field of representation is comprehension. When motion stops, comprehension finito.

CHRISTOPHE CHERIX: IN A GAME WHERE YOU ARE SUPPOSED TO HAVE THE MAXIMUM "FREEDOM", YOU HAVE CUT ANY POSSIBILITY OF IT. IS THAT A METAPHOR OF YOUR OWN ARTISTIC CONDITION, IN THE SAME WAY AS YOU SAID BEFORE THAT YOU "HAD TO MAKE" VIDEOS OR PAINTINGS?

There is no freedom. Art is interesting because you are never free, because you are under specific conditions.

LIONEL BOVIER: BUT ISN'T IT PRECISELY THE KIND OF SITUATION IN WHICH, AS IN A VIDEOGAME, YOU SHOULD LOOK FOR A FAILURE IN THE SYSTEM ?

Beauty is the failure! I mean by being a painter, I also know that when you come close to beauty you are on a verge of failure. As an individual one should not look for qualities but for the loss of them all. That's also the line that separates the artist from a philosopher. The philosopher knows about beauty but avoids it. The artist doesn't avoid beauty, rather he prefers to become a human mistake. Plato considered artists as low figures in the hierarchy of his ideal society because they deal with real objects and simulation; while the philosopher is treating the ideas that define reality. When you are making art, you are always accumulating qualities: beauty, success, experience, and so on, instead of reaching the state of abstraction, essence and ideas. Look at Picasso, the guy wearing shorts on the beach and trying to sleep with as many girls as he can, he has the same kind of agenda for paintings: accumulating more and more experiments with forms.

CHRISTOPHE CHERIX: STARTING FROM THIS PHILOSOPHICAL PREMISE, HOW DID YOU BECOME INTERESTED IN SUCH FORMAL ISSUES AS PAINTING?

My identity is to work with philosophical tools, but my attraction in art would be to access the ability of, say, John Armleder. The video *Soft Driller* (1994) was about that kind of paradoxical and desperate artistic position: one guy saying that he will fuck up the other and this one constantly denying this perspective: both sides of my own position. That's why I am working with machines that were built to help us, but finally end up complicating our entire life as they become mirror sites of it. This room is packed with computers and electronics and that's something that I'm not comfortable with. It's like women.

JOHN TREMBLAY: BUT YOU ARE NOT SURROUNDED BY WOMEN...

No, but Vanessa embodies them all...

JOHN TREMBLAY: WHICH IS PRECISELY WHAT SHE IS UP TO IN HER PERFORMANCES, USING ALL DIFFERENT TYPE OF CHARACTERS TO DELEGATE HERSELF TO THE AUDIENCE...

LIONEL BOVIER: YOU SAID THAT, BEFORE THIS YEAR, YOU COULD NOT CONTEXTUALIZE YOUR OWN WORK. HOW DID IT HAPPEN THAT YOU NOW SEEM ABLE TO DO IT?

In a way, painting was the point I had to reach to be able to have a perspective on my work. In the process of oil painting on canvas, you apply layers of memory on a projection surface and you end up with a kind of window. David Robbins once said that «wall painting is a door and a painting on canvas a window.»

LIONEL BOVIER: AND WHAT ABOUT SIZE?

Size is not important. Pollock made bigger paintings and the museums just became bigger... that's all about size.

PPP: an interview

PPP* IS A SHOW AT REBECCA CAMHI GALLERY IN ATHENS...

It is a show about portable computers and videogames.

BUT JUST A FEW PEOPLE IN THE ART WORLD HAVE ANY COMPUTING EXPERIENCE AND EVEN LESS OF THEM HAVE EVER PLAYED ANY VIDEOGAME. DO YOU THINK THAT YOU WILL HAVE ANY PUBLIC?

They will find their connections, there are some intelligent people in the Arts you know! But let's give here some descriptions. Portable computers are machines that keep in their storage your photos, your thoughts and your calculations – so you are able to always carry with you the world of your choice. Conservative people try to sell computers as if they were necessary tools. They suggest them for what you can do with them, but I love them mostly for their handicaps. They are capable of a certain amount of memory, after that they freeze. They also speak a language in between their own and the one of their users, which is imperfect and ever changing. They are a great contemporary landscape for an artist, even if themselves have nothing to do with art. They are as much related with art as psychoanalysis is related with anxiety disorder. You cannot cure anxiety disorder with analysis, it is beyond its power. In the same way, we will not renovate art with computers but still, they are ideal objects for representation. They can even be used as role models, because computers can teach you how to live and watch.

BUT WHY DO YOU CHOOSE TO REPRESENT THEM USING THE LANGUAGE OF PAINTING? WHY NOT TAKE A PHOTO, OR MAKE A MOVIE OR EVEN PUT SOME POWERBOOK TOGETHER IN A BIG TRANSPARENT CONTAINER OR SOMETHING?

Because whatever you may paint with oil on canvas, will join the company of famous characters: Jesus and his Mother painted by Rafael, Marat by David, Olympia by Ingres and Manet, Marilyn Monroe by Andy Warhol, the American Flag by Jasper Johns. Now, this looks to me a nice company for a Powerbook and a Sony PlayStation.

WHAT IS A PLAYSTATION?

It's a console that you plug into your TV set. It's a very theatrical experience, and you control your hero with a stick. You turn the stick right or left and the hero walks to his adventures. A famous hero today is SuperMario by Nintendo 64.

I SEE! THAT GUY WHO LOOKS LIKE A PLUMPER WITH THE RED HAT. IN YOUR PPP SHOW IN ATHENS, YOU HAVE HIM IN A VIDEO NEXT TO YOUR PAINTING. WHY?

In that video, he sleeps all the time. I thought that it would be nice have him sleep next to a painting. Of course the art is only at the canvas, that video is there just as a friend.

BUT DO YOU LIKE HIS FACE? AND THAT MUSTACHE!

You come to like the hero that you have to play. I believe that reality is not just what exists. Reality is what we are used to watch, and in this sense even SuperMario can be emblematic of reality.

WHY ALL THAT INTEREST FOR CARTOONS? ALL COMPUTER GAME HEROES ARE NOTHING BUT CARTOONS. WHY NOT TO FOCUS ON THE IMAGES OF REAL PEOPLE?

When you want to meet real people today, you can choose between visiting a person in her house or a place like a street or a bar, or you can just sit in front of your computer, log on the Internet and meet different people in a chat room. Soon, we may dress as SuperMario or as a Dragon, and meet a Prince in a 3D animated forest. Which will be our real face then? The one that we will still encounter every morning in our mirror or the one that we will use online? In a cartoon World, our exterior is something like a car, you can have it big and black or red and small.

It's great because you can observe forms without being obliged to defend the form that you happen to have.

AND WHAT ABOUT CONTEMPORARY ART?

Poor contemporary art... But I don't care that much about it. Do you?

* PPP comes from Point to Point Protocol. Can be also used for Painting and Photography Protocol.

Miltos Manetas, 1998

Moving and Shooting

A: Contemporary Art museums are terrible!

B: WHY?

A: What we call Contemporary Art, which is nothing but an elite sequel to Modern Art, is strongly based on the sensation of "displacement". To realize such a displacement, contemporary artists usually employ a few basic tricks. The most common of these tricks is multiplying an image and changing its scale.

B: HOW DOES THAT WORK?

A: It works because the art is exhibited in empty interiors. The idea of using empty space to help manipulate emotions goes back to the invention of perspective, in the times of the Italian Renaissance. Using perspective's laws, you can make an image that does not include yourself. Instead, your position will be the so-called vanishing point; which is somewhere outside of the picture, similar to how God can be absent from its creation. In more recent times, Dadaists and their friends stopped framing real space, breaking the picture and reintroducing perspective. They did so by putting their objects in position and by applying metaphorical sense upon them. Ready-made, and similar, objects are entirely different from any sculpture, yet are still connected to the idea of painting.

B: REALLY?

A: You cannot appreciate a bottle holder or a bicycle wheel until you have them "framed" with empty space. Even the existence of simple furniture in a room disorients the viewer from having that exact amount of displacement that would lead him to exclaim, "This is an artwork! It is great!"

B: WHAT DO YOU MEAN BY "EMPTY SPACE?"

A: Wide open empty interior space was not always available. In fact, it came with the modern times, along with the realization that everything on the surface of Earth has been discovered, and that our planet is nothing but a giant ready-made planet which we can observe from an available moon. It suddenly became evident that a naked room was now the only place where you can hide yourself. An empty room (four white walls) became the context. There you could make some magic spell, like Joseph Beuys; you could change something into nothing, or even nothing into something. However, in that empty room, you would still meet people and socialize.

B: DO YOU MEAN HAVING PARTIES?

A: Artists and their friends began enjoying their privileges, and in the last fifty years (1950-1999) they created a society, along with a small, but nice, niche market. In this new situation, the artist became the person that makes the discoveries.Together with his gallerist, he would invite other friends and foes to see the exhibits. Soon people without talent, but with the experience of May 68 (Germano Celant's generation) joined the game.

They quickly convinced some of their old pals, now successful politicians, that this adventure could somehow be profitable. With the combination of public money and private funds, the friends of the artists (curators) started housing the most awarded discoveries inside of museums, institutes and foundations. As the market value of the discoveries and the power of the curators increased, the fame and reputation of these institutions overtook the fame and reputation of even the most successful galleries. And why not? Museums were the emptiest, widest, and whitest of all the spaces!

B: AHA!

A: Before Contemporary Art existed, museums were great. In the cities of our passive world, they would function as virtual reality machines. They would transport you quickly and inexpensively to the most bizarre past, or future. They were full of items both disconnected from our time and expelled by their times. A Roman sculpture, a Chinese vase, and a Cézanne painting were not where you would expect them to be: in a Roman courtyard, in a Chinese kitchen, or over the sofa in a Frenchman's house. Instead, they were positioned in alien displays and were brought together under the same walls, within walking distance from one another. The museum would transform all of its contents! I bet that, provided the guards are asleep, if someone took his clothes off in the museum, nobody would object. People would exist there not as citizens, but as visitors. They were not supposed to watch each other. But Contemporary Art museums changed everything. They activated empty space, made a context out of it. They turned any old object from the past or present into a concept.

B: I GOT IT! BUT IS IT FUN?

A: Not really. Sex is fun. Moving into an unknown terrain, looking around and discovering places can also be fun. Today, you can do that with your fingers in front of a computer! New land appears on your screen while you are connected online. Or while you play a videogame. It is a nice and clean land created by pixels. You can be there with other humans, but mostly, you are alone. This way, it feels private, as nature is to an Aborigine. Each game you play is a new experience, teaching you some recent patterns of moving, and of exploring reality.

A videogame makes us enjoy life twice. We take pleasure from the reality of the game, when pushing a button to open a door. And then, after we quit and come back to the world outside where a door can be opened in an analogue way, we enjoy that old door as well. The same type of psychological confusion exists when we visit Venice for a day, and then fly back to a big noisy city. The difference between the two worlds makes both desirable.

B: YEAH...

A: Another thing that we really enjoy is destruction. It is again a matter of visibility. We want to break the appearance, in order to see how something is composed, or just turn everything into pieces as we move. In real life, the combination of moving and firing a gun can be a dangerous sport, while in a videogame, it is safe to perform violence. In shoot-em-all (or shoot-em-up) videogames, such as Doom and Quake, a chair may fall into pieces, but it may also stay there, indestructible. Destruction in a videogame is less predictable than in reality. By using the proper cheats, you can cross through walls, or get unlimited ammo. Shooting becomes natural, simply another bodily function. You will still meet enemies, but the cheat of immortality will save you from the boring rules of death. In the videogame version of reality, you are free to avoid death.

This is what makes computer games as empty, as interesting, and as abstract as art. Videogames, like art, ignore the user, even though they would not be able to function without him.

B: YES. OKAY. SHALL WE PLAY SOME SUPER MARIO BROS. NOW?

A: I cannot. I am busy...

Written in 1999 for the show *Museum Meltdown* (Moderna Museet, Stockholm, Sweden, May 22 – August 19, 1999), by Palle Torsson & Tobias Bernstrup.

NEEN manifesto

A Few Things I Know about NEEN

NEEN stands for Neensters, a still undefined generation of visual artists. Some of them belong to the contemporary art world, while others are software creators, web designers, and videogame directors and animators.

Our official theories about reality, such as quantum physics, have proved that the taste of our life is the taste of a simulation. Machines help us feel comfortable with this condition, as they simulate the simulation that we call nature. Opening the door of your room, or clicking on a folder on your computer's desktop, will send you to similar destinations. These are two versions of reality that are seemingly perfect and dense, but they will start dissolving after you analyze them.

Computing is to NEEN what fantasy was to surrealism, and what freedom was to communism. Computing creates its context, but it can also be postponed. Neensters buy the newest products and they study how to create momentum. They glorify machines, but they get easily bored with them. Sometimes they simply prefer to watch others operating them.

Neensters find their pleasure in the in-betweens of actions. NEEN is about losing time on different operating systems.

Neensters love copying, in a similar, but slightly different way that the city of Hong Kong multiplies its most successful buildings. Names, clothes, style, art, and architecture are important for Neensters. So they create all of these things from scratch, as if what has been done before is not important. NEEN is very sentimental, but it is not about identity, even though Neensters do occasionally use their identities as passwords in order to get certain privileges.

Because the identity of a Neenster is in his state of mind, he is free to use the identity of another Neenster if he needs to do so. But this works also in reverse, as a Neenster can create artwork for another Neenster. That is the major difference between NEEN and Contemporary Art.

While in Contemporary Art you need to be yourself all the time, a certain type of hero that is always polishing his image until he becomes a mirror of his lifetime, in NEEN you are a kind of screen. A Neenster projects a temporary self that is always under construction, and that moves from the present to the past and future, without limitations.

Because a Neenster publishes everything on the web, his state of mind reflects the public taste. Neensters are public personae.

If fantasy brought Surrealists to the ridiculous, and revolution drove communists to failure, it will be curious to observe where computing will bring NEEN.

Miltos Manetas, New York 2000.

www.afterneen.com

Save As...

On the third day, Jesus returned to the earth, having risen from the dead. In the Gospel according to Mark (16:12), he is said to have appeared to his apostles "in another form." This is probably why Caravaggio, in his famous painting *The Supper in Emmaus*, did not paint Jesus with a beard, but rather clean-shaven.

A clean-shaven Jesus is a slightly different Jesus. Like a picture that you open in Photoshop and "Save As" a JPG for the web, Jesus returned in a new format, a version which was lighter, and easier for people to use. If he lost some pixels during the compression, this was merely a necessity. According to his church, his mission was to become a universal standard and it seems that for that purpose, full quality should not really matter.

Imagine Nature (or God) as a stubborn old man making infinite variations of all sorts of things. A long time ago God made a piece of hardware (the Multiverse), and loaded it with some basic software (Life). After he installed a bit of RAM (Time), God let the simulation start.

Maybe God was trying to create a self-portrait. Maybe he recalled that once he was young and beautiful, and he desired to see that beauty again.

But God is not an artist, so he has not been restricted to a specific format. He started producing different versions of reality, one on top of the other. He tried all the buttons and all the combinations. His Multiverse hardware acquired so much experience, that it was barely hardware any more. The Multiverse could now automatically produce new slots and install RAM (Time) on itself. As a consequence, RAM (Time) became intelligent.

Time sometimes behaves as real, and sometimes as virtual. Sometimes you feel it, sometimes you do not. If you push Time, it may crash, but if you push it just a little harder, you may succeed in running very sophisticated applications simultaneously.

Choose Expand

"There are also many other things which Jesus did, and if they should be written every one, I suppose that even the world itself would not contain the books needed to be written." (John 21:25)

In certain possible universes, fiction is the user. The real purpose for everything is literature. People are just a medium. They come in a portfolio of about a hundred different prints, in editions of one hundred and fifty signed copies. Post-human literary agents eventually acquire these portfolios, and over time, they are positioned in different geographic locations and civilizations. But people have intelligence, and therefore are constantly searching for the other members of their original portfolio.

People think that they must connect with others because of their shared portfolio memories, so when they find them, they create relationships. This is how stories between people are happening. Sometimes, people recognize their own copies. When this happens, they want to find (and affect) all of the missing companions, all of the portfolios containing their copies. This desire adds a sense of tragedy and continuation to their destiny. This desire also fuels a person's entrance in the public life, where that person, starts exclaiming his own theories.

As more people redirect their actions from the personal domain to the public one, theories multiply. If you try to describe all of them, the Universe will turn into a hypothetical Universe. This is a danger that God would do anything to avoid. So, a protective software was long ago installed in the human soul. This software obliges us to produce theories always in different formats. And as a DVD player does not read a VHS tape, only theories which become a standard and are transported into newer formats survive. All of the rest becomes obsolete.

But for some of their beloved theories, people create emulators. Take Marxism, for example. Once a very famous theory of the twentieth century, it's now emulated and transmitted via its alien operating system of the Internet. The original theories in their old formats may still be interesting as "collector's items", but a busy and productive user wouldn't care much for such items. Ashes to ashes, dust to dust...

If Jesus was to return today, he shouldn't simply come back clean-shaven, he should manifest himself instead like a giant Pokémon.

First published in *EMIGRE#57,* February 2001.

E-mail

Sent on 12-20-2001

From Rebecca:

Are you mad at me? Where is the little hello – the little sign of love?

xx Rebecca

To Rebecca:

I am not mad. I just prefer dry and impersonal e-mails. It is as if we are speaking to each other from inside our bodies, without greetings and signs of any kind.

Like if we are many in one. We can do that through e-mail. We can save our tenderness for later, for when we meet in real life, or for some special e-mail affection intended as a bonus.

xxx

Miltos

The Fourfortyfour Theory

Sometimes, when we look at the time on our phone, or on our computer, we have what I would call a "4:44", pronounced "four forty-four moment". This moment can be achieved at certain intervals, such as: 0:00, 0:12, 01:01, 1:11, 1:23, 02:02, 2:22, 2:34, 03:03, 3:33, 3:45, 4:04, 4:44, 4:56, 05:05, 5:55, 06:06, 07:07, 08:08, 09:09, 10:10, 11:11, 12:12, 12:34, 13:11, 13:13, 14:22, 14:14, 15:15, 16:16, 17:17, 18:18, 19:19, 20:20, 21:21, 22:22, 23:23.

These numbers, which look very nice, are islands created by time. People accidentally get into these moments from different places all over the planet, and just stay there in the moments for that minute. Whenever we have the same 4:44 moment, then we are together within a mental place. This place is so "mental" that the moment moves through time according to our location. For example, when it is 4:44 A.M. in New York, it is 1:44 A.M. in Los Angeles, and when it is 4:44 A.M. in Los Angeles, it is 7:44 A.M. in New York.

4:44 theory is NEEN and therefore, the theory does not explain anything about these special moments, but rather it draws attention to them, as NEEN is for drawing attention and not for providing explanation. The theory is also concerned with some special existential crises, such as, "I just arrived in L.A. from N.Y. and I have not yet changed the time on my computer. So if I am to encounter a 4:44 moment on the computer, is that moment still valid?" Such a question might seem silly, but since the question deals with the very contemporary problem of location, it is a valid one. The theory is concerned with the question of where am I when I am "on my computer"? If we accept the 4:44 moment as genuine, and it is genuine of course, because any 4:44 moment that we encounter is by definition, genuine, then we should also start thinking of where we are in terms of local place (and in local time). When we are connected, we are somewhere that may be separate from our local place.

Miltos Manetas, Los Angeles, 2002

www.fourfortyfour.com

Websites are the Art of our Times

Websites are Today's Most Radical and Important Art Objects

The Internet is not just another "medium", as the old media insist that it is, but it is mostly a "space", similar to the American continent immediately after it was discovered, as anything that can be found on the Web has a physical presence and occupies some kind of real estate. Encountering a logo, a picture or an animation on the Internet is a totally different experience than finding the same stuff in a magazine or on television.

"Things" on the Internet exist in a specific location, while in magazines, and on television, these contents are mostly bullets of information. Online they constitute a body; they are parts of a new genre. They are web entities. These "creatures" are often a mix of humans and software such as Google, but sometimes they are composed entirely by information. Such as is the case of Googlism.com, a website that is able to make a portrait of anything by collecting descriptions about that subject from Google [1].

Most web entities are also social entities. They get in touch and advertise their existence to each other. Similar to how human beings act, they will evaluate, criticize, "link" to each other, and ultimately, develop a "taste".

Bob Dobbs (a friend of Marshall McLuhan) said that "advertising is communication between machines". He also suggested that machines came alive in 1967, and that "now they are in an angelic state". According to Mr. Dobbs, advertising is "communication between angels".

Some of these Web Entities – or shall we simply call them Angels? – communicate with us and also between them in a "pretty" way. As a result, a new type of art, or what later may be called art, can be found in certain websites. But where exactly?

In the Telic Spirit

The Web is nothing more and nothing less than what the World has always been: unvisited and unfriendly territories that are gradually transformed into a domestic landscape. From the Alps to the Japanese garden, the scenario is the illusory promise of order and system. But still, the simple rocks and sand in the well-arranged composition of a Japanese garden, for a better-trained intellect, are pure black holes and chaos.

The Web emerged from this chaos; in a certain way it came directly out of the Trojan Horse and now we are all Ulysses, lost at sea. But like Ulysses, we are not traveling alone. There is a special spirit that helps us navigate: the spirit of Telic.

Telos, in Greek, means "the end" or "the purpose". Telic is described as "something directed or tending towards a goal or purpose; purposeful". "I am driving my car to Los Angeles" is a Telic statement, while "I am driving my car" is not, as there is no destination. Telic is our relationship with the tools that help us to design the World, and helps us to see things in perspective. Telic is in mobile phones and computers, and even in the way our houses and clothes are manufactured. Our times are Telic.

Telic firmly advertises itself even if it's not really certain (one may never arrive in Los Angeles, but crash on a tree or something). Telic is serious. It tries to explain every little detail. It will submit footnotes and references. It's also over-creative, often in a paranoid way.

Telic does not have a taste. It can be as ugly as an IBM computer. Telic authors and artists usually have jobs in the technology industry, or they are teachers in universities. They survive thanks to the grants that other Telic people manage and they avoid the art world, which in return, ignores them.

But Telic shapes the World. As J.G. Ballard wrote, "Science and technology multiply around us. To an increasing extend they dictate the languages in which we speak and think. Either we use those languages or we remain mute".

Telic is the art of making sense from these languages. But then again, do we really want to make sense? Why are we doomed to be so domesticated and so productive? You wish for there to be a secret society, some people who know how to give you the feelings directly and who will keep you thinking, even after you quit browsing. You wish there were websites that could offer you the metaphysical suspense of a painting. You wish for NEEN.

NEEN is a State of Mind

> "I actually know for sure that there are scenes on the Internet that nobody knows about and nobody cares about, and within those milieus, very specialized sensibilities are evolving". William Gibson, 2003 [2]

In 2001, a group of people from all around the planet started talking about NEEN. These people eventually met, some online and some in the real world, and started exchanging their experiences. A new art movement was born, the first movement of the twenty-first Century. NEEN is still mainly a concept, and as such, it has its own life, one that is independent from the activity of people that practice it. NEEN is the crazy little brother of Telic. It owes its existence to the realization that certain ideas or animations, certain sounds, words or behaviors, are indeed NEEN.

A person that thinks about NEEN is a Neenster. What a Neenster does may sometimes seem silly, but only because it is easy and amazing. A Neenster is not trying to make sense, as he/she does not suffer from any stress of production and does not follow a pattern. The dream of a Neenster is to become an Icon, but a special kind of one, not the type of Icon you usually find in the glossies and in the art magazines. A Neenster starts his career by becoming the Icon of his own imagination. Then he projects that Icon to the outside, as if the Icon were fact.

Identity is not a priority for a Neenster, but one will fetishize oneself anyway, and use that as a style. This is a fast way to produce content. In contrast with contemporary artists, a Neenster will change identities often, according to the situations. Neen is ultimately a state of mind. People such as Lucio Fontana, who was painting by simply slashing a canvas, were NEEN before NEEN even existed.

Because the Internet is the best place to exercise inertia, Neensters spend a lot of time online. Unlike the Telics, Neensters are friends of the information and not its "users". Neensters are obsessed with names. They will run a search on the Internet to see if the domain with a new name they have envisioned is available. If it is available, they will register it. Immediately afterwards, they will create something fresh and put it online. It will be something minimal, strange, and romantic.

Neensters will make web pages that are a new *object d'art*, which is what we are looking for when we surf the Internet.

It's Really Interesting... (Is it Jeffrey?) [3]

"Contemporary Art", the Art of the Past Century, was based mostly on the following a principle: "if you put something in an empty room, it seems strange and significant". A variation was: "if you take something out of its context, it seems strange and significant". Another was: "if you change the scale of something, it will seem strange and significant". The last one: "if you multiply something, it also becomes strange and significant".

But after eighty years of different combinations of any kinds of objects inside the hopelessly empty spaces of our art institutions, nothing seems really interesting. We see clearly now that the "art" is simply a bunch of trash, just some products to be bought from a mall.

Outside of the Internet, there is no glory. Non-Internet artists are freelance employees of other employees, (the curators of the exhibitions). Institutions bestow curators with confidence and power. They are not supposed to look for any unseen objects, but for some evidence of human expression, which they will bring back to their commissioners, in the way a well-trained dog would do with its ball. Exhibitions are identity-control tests. The exhibitions are not creating anything new, they are just sampling stories.

No wonder then that top-level art exhibitions, such as the Whitney Biennial, the Documenta in Kassel, the Manifesta, or the Venice Biennial, look like Graduation Day for Anthropology students. In these "shows", any realistic representation could as well be used as an illustration for the *National Geographic*, while any abstract piece becomes mere decoration.

The Art World is relaxed and open to anything, just because it knows that nothing peculiar will ever happen. Even if the gallery is left empty, the public will search for the label with the name of the artist who did the "work", and they will find satisfaction in one way or another. Beds, balloons and chickens: real space has lost its emptiness. On the Internet, where space is created by software and random imagination, an empty webpage is really empty. People and Web Entities (Angels) still invent unpredictable objects to fill the space.

Collectors

Because Art is ultimately the power to put a form in the chaos, anyone who is busy with forms and concepts is an artist. That today includes "curators", "gallerists", "museum people" and even "collectors". They are all artists, most of them bad, but artists.

A "collector" however also does another job. Because he is a man with property, he decides what should survive. That's his artistic media after all: the power of keeping a piece in existence. Never has this power been more significant, than for a collector of websites.

Very few people are cool enough to collect websites. It requires intuition and courage. It is similar to the purchase of an apartment in a ghetto area of Harlem. You need to take the risks. Anybody instead can walk into a Gagosian gallery and buy some contemporary art. It's as easy as buying designer clothes: the House which sells the product guarantees its value and you get what you pay for: a giant certificate of authenticity with some picture on the front.

When you buy "Contemporary Art", you buy a copy of what already belongs to a Museum, because contemporary art museums are made specifically for this type of art and will eventually host anything produced by the major galleries.

It's an industry of memorabilia. Collecting in this case is not an adventure, but a banal experience, something like opening yet another Savings Account. Larry Gagosian in fact, refers with surprising sincerity to his collectors as "customers". It is OK, of course, to be a customer, but it is far more interesting and courageous to be a collector of websites.

The collector of a website has total control on the pieces he owns because the art in a website is not the animation or the code or the pictures that the website contains, but the experience of all the above in a unique place somewhere in cyberspace, under a unique name. What a collector of websites acquires, is a contract that passes to him the ownership of the web domain – the place where the work actually exists. If he decides one day to not pay the hosting fee, the work will disappear. You can burn a painting but its photograph will always allow people to reproduce it. It's not the same with the website though. The name of the website will return to the pool of the available domain names. The whole piece will expire, as if it has never existed.

Collecting a website, is a trip to a secret Villa. If a collector decides to keep this experience just to himself, he may put a password on the page and nobody will be able to access it. He will lock the Villa and keep the art a secret and that is OK. But if he decides to let the piece be available for viewing to the public, he will experience the feelings of the ultimate property.

You are the owner of an art that all can enjoy but only you own. In a time where anyone can buy anything, the only really glamorous collecting is the collecting of websites and other digital objects. The pieces which are not considered art yet but will become art later.

Miltos Manetas, 2002 – 2004

[1] www.googlism.com
[2] Eric S. Elkins, [Interview with William Gibson], in *Underground Online*, undated. Online at the URL
www.ugo.com/channels/freestyle/features/williamgibson/.
[3] Jeffrey Deitch (ed), *Everything That's Interesting is New. The Dakis Joannou Collection*, Cantz/Deste Foundation for Contemporary Art, 1996.

Better Than a Painter (for Angelo Plessas)

Portraiture is an art, and it is one of the main opportunities for human expression. A portrait is an interpretation of our peers. It is a method that fixes our opinion, or our view of others on the blackboard of the present, and on the undulating wall of the future.

A portrait can also be a written story of someone's acts, and photographs and movies are always intended to be portraits, even if they rarely succeed. But until today, the highest accomplishment in portraiture was made through painting.

As an apple is not an apple when you paint its image, the face of a person is not that person, but something that belongs to her aura. Or, more precisely, something that belongs to the shadow of her aura. A painted portrait is a field of influence and possibility. In the latter half of the previous century, Flash animation came into existence. Flash animation was a newer and better than any oil on canvas technique of portraiture. These animations, or *quasi*-animations, are based on a picture or a drawing, but some of them are simply abstractions. When seen from outside the context of the Internet, they lose some of their glamour. The very existence of a domain name on the top of them, and the fact that you have to write that name on a browser to call them up, serves to extend the fiction, while at the same time gives them the authority of Realism.

As happens with any new modus operandi, only a few creators have the courage and the determination to use Flash animation in order to create important art. Angelo Plessas is one of these few. It is not a surprise then, that only a few observers can understand his genius, and they prefer to consider him a "designer". But anyway, they still call Yves Saint Laurent and Vivian Westwood, "designers" just as they call Andrei Tarkovsky and Francis Ford Coppola "directors" as if it would ever be possible to "design" or "direct" the mystery that these creators know how to manipulate.

Angelo Plessas began his work with a self portrait. He painted, or rather Flash animated himself, as the center of a circular Internet Explorer window, for the website aroundmyself.com. He continued making websites for other people, every time capturing their essence and sometimes – whenever possible – their future essence. Plessas, never acting as a designer (which in my opinion is a pejorative term that denotes a job and a client), created portraits of the Italian artist Vanessa Beecroft (vanessabeecroft.com), British composer gnac (marktranmer.com) and Neen entrepreneur Jan Åman (janaman.com). The important and glamorous citizens of the previous century would have their portraits done by the likes of Helmut Newton, Annie Leibovitz and Timothy Greenfield-Sanders. But today, if you are somebody of note, the best person to capture your vanity, is Angelo Plessas.

Rafaël Rozendaal

Rafaël Rozendaal was born in Amsterdam the 6th of June, 1980. His father is a painter, and his background is very religious: a Calvinist Dutch farm life. Rozendaal's mother was a fashion journalist in Paris and studied architecture. She is from Brazil, and her grandfather, Humberto Castello Branco, was the President of Brazil in the 60s, a kind of a dictator. He died in a plane crash. They never figured out if that was just an accident or a political statement. It makes a nice contrast: a Dutch modest hard working side of the family and a Brazilian spoiled upper-class presidential side.

To get a fresh impression of Rafaël Rozendaal, here is his self-portrait: his websites up to now:

whitetrash.nl,

iamveryverysorry.com,

bestkeptsecretintheworld.com,

everythingyouseeisinthepast.com,

afterlinks.com,

wewillattack.com,

stagnationmeansdecline.com.

Rafaël Rozendaal succeeds somehow to absorb contemporary art but keeps himself unspoiled from infomercials. I've seen him recently opening an issue of *Artforum* with genuine surprise. «Don't you know this magazine?», I asked him. «No», he replied. How rare!

It was the night of his opening at the Electronic Orphanage in Los Angeles. Two giant hands were projected on the screen, against a red background. There was a mouse for the public to click. I feel too embarrassed to describe what happens when you click on one of those hands. It's not "nice", as the title suggests. Check it out at

misternicehands.com.

Is this art? Surely not, most of the people who were present that night at the EO decided. But it's not a cartoon either. Somehow it leaves you with a strong impression. And its not even funny.

My favorite piece by him is a Flash animation he did for the WhitneyBiennial.com, where the user can delete clouds endlessly. But his very best piece is

wewillattack.com.

Again, there is no way to describe this piece. Is this what makes Rafaël Rozendaal a Neenstar? Maybe it would be better to let him "talk". The following text is from a recent e-mail that he sent to me.

«If you sneeze on your screen you see the different RGB parts of colors: the drops make you look behind the screen.»

«There was a time when paint had to be handmade and therefore painters were restricted to studios. When oil paint was first sold in tubes, there were two kinds of artists: those who embraced the new found freedom and those who rejected it. The latter stayed in their perfectly controlled studio environment, because they liked their old-fashioned blend of paint and they did not trust the new technology: paint from a tube can't be good cause it's too easy. But the tubes pushed radical artists to places they had never been before and out into the open. To lakes, forests, cafes, farms and whorehouses. Good artists embrace their times and are not afraid of trying new things.»

«I know many people, both designers and artists who use the computer every day for years and still think of it as a tool. These people surf the web to find scraps to fill real space, but can not see the web as world of its own. My computer, is not a tool, it's a space, a world, a landscape. It's screen has more dimensions than real life: in a browser window you can look further than in a real window.»

«You cannot lose yourself into an artwork if tourists and screaming children are running around in a museum. The web is the most intimate stage for art so far. The internet is a place you cannot touch and therefore it touches you. A world behind glass, like a present waiting to be opened but you cant. A place between imagination and real life, between thoughts and objects.»

«Sleeping is very neen: you defragment your thoughts, you clean your hard drive. Insomnia is a very telic state of mind: you feel guilty to relax. I like neen cause I never asked for it to happen, it was there waiting for me.»

«I see my work as something close to painting: you move the parts around until there's a tension, a friction. The pieces are moving, but there's no beginning or end, a place between moment and motion. its like trembling, like hot air that changes your view and makes you lose focus. You use parts to create the work and hope for it to become alive, to transport itself and start to live a life of its own in the public domain.»

«The void is beauty, something that doesn't fit, something that should not be there, something that is out of place. it doesn't add up.»

Miltos Manetas interviewed Rafaël Rozendaal for *Purple Magazine* in 2003.

Manifesto of Art After Videogames

We call them "videogames" but these games are not made for video recorders. Videogames are made for computers, and because of that, they are not "games". Or at least, they are not just games: I believe that videogames are instead, extended versions of reality. The process that started with the poems of Homer, Mahabharata and the Bible, continues now through videogames.

According to the Christian religion, **God** got very upset when people started multiplying themselves. But then he went mad when he realized that they were also having fun while doing it. So **God** expelled people from his paradise and later had to send his own avatar to bring some of us back. Apparently, like a television without a Playstation connected to it, a paradise without people was a very lonely place. From their side, people, who were conceived as **God**'s mirror-images, discovered from very early how to mirror themselves. They would do so not only by facts (sex), but also by words (fantasy). At this point, **God** was really in trouble: while a human creature – the product of love making – is a mortal, a fantasy hero such as **Ulysses**, **Supermario**, **Buddha** and **Jesus** can be immortal.

Anyway, after some serious research, people found out that the appearance of the World is nothing but an illusion and they decided to build a few other worlds and to compete with **God**'s "corporate" illusion. That illusion is supported mainly by what we call Reality.

But how exactly does reality look like? "Can you show it to me?" someone said... Reality isn't certain, cold is not cold for whoever wears a warm uniform and the night is not dark if you are supplied with a few laser visors. Still, our consideration of cold and darkness survives... The (fake) information of "reality" is nothing but a very bad operating system. To get rid of it and "calculate" the World successfully, we start emulating **God's** creative process. We start building creatures ourselves, creatures that should be able to write down their own story, paint their self-portrait and record the sounds around them. At some point, these creatures should become capable to compare themselves with us. To start, such creatures should have their own feelings; and to start building such creatures, we invented videogames.

A videogame character isn't just the cartoon we see on the screen. The complete character is a combined creature: it's that cartoon together with the Player. It is the Player's energy what "powers" the puppet: in

SuperMario, if you don't play with him, the hero falls asleep." Mario", is nobody else but you.

Or, the "New You."

In the Nintendo 64 game, **SuperMario** starts his adventures by throwing himself inside paintings. By doing so, he enters a scenario and collects some experience. When he is exhausted, he doesn't die, but he returns to the castle where these paintings are hanging. There he can relax and think about what to do next. The game is a multi-leveled experience, exciting but also boring like our "real life".

But of course, a videogame is after all a commercial product and its revelatory power is limited. Feelings – which could be direct and simple – are complex and confused. Purpose takes over and at that point, beauty collapses into entertainment.

What started as our opportunity to create a new species made by humans merged with cartoons, becomes just another page from the script of *The Society of the Spectacle*. The only way to save our relationship with videogames, is to exercise the Zen of Non-Playing. By Doing so, we become Artists After Videogames.

An artist who works with videogames shouldn't create or change anything. He/she should only extract the hidden notion of the game, by looking carefully at the parade of symbols the game is offering already. An explosion should be captured and turned into a Turner-like landscape. Our relationship with a monster should become somehow romantic: instead of shooting it, we should start taking photos.

A Painter doesn't eat a piece of bread but paints it. An Artist after Videogames doesn't create a videogame, but copies it.

Miltos Manetas, 2004.

The Square. (4 Art trends)

Looking back at the arts and lifestyle of the last ten years, I can see four distinct trends:

1. "Beige" (the name is coined by Olivier Zahm and Elein Fleiss, the founders of the Purple Institute in Paris).

2. "Relational Aesthetics" (the name is coined by the writer and curator Nicolas Bourriaud).

3. "Telic" (coined by Lexicon Branding after a commission by myself, asking for a term to represent computer-related art and creativity).

4. "Neen" (coined by Lexicon Branding after a commission by myself, asking for a term to represent computer-related art and creativity).

Beige starts with Araki and ends with Vanessa Beecroft. It includes people such as the photographers Terry Richardson and Wolfgang Tillmans, the directors Sophia Coppola and Gus Van Sant, the rock group Sonic Youth, faux-writer J.T Leroy [1] and "his" friend Asia Argento, fashion icon Kate Moss, certain brands such as Comme Des Garcons, Cosmic Wonder, Bless and Undercover as well as many young Japanese photographers and fashion editors. Beige is about feelings that are properly "human," such as love, despair and vanity. These feelings were with us even before computers but the fact that the computers of the 80s and 90s were mostly beige, is significant. Beige, a color that is neither black nor white, is about young people, their love and loneliness, the way we crash sometimes into the wall of the everyday. Beige is the aesthetic of the snapshots we take while we are crashing into that wall.

Relational Aesthetics starts with Guy Debord and ends with Maurizio Cattelan. It's about a type of art cultivated in art schools and turned – with the assistance of art curators – into an international art language. A "Relational Aestetist," such as artists Philippe Parreno, Pierre Huyghe, Liam Gillick or Rirkrit Tiravanija, is usually a highly professional and serious artist, even when he makes jokes. "Today's artist appears as an operator of signs, modeling production structures so as to provide significant doubles. An entrepreneur/politician/director" Bourriaud writes [2]. Fashion designer Martin Margiela is one of the few designers with the conceptual vigor of a Relational Aestetist: in all of his shows, his assistants are dressed in white tunics to resemble medical workers.

Telic covers pretty much everything that has to do with technology. You find much of it in the *Wired Magazine* but it's not only about computers, Telic is everywhere. The term Telic comes from the Greek word Telos (the end) and means something with a specific destination. Under Telic we find all kinds of cool and not so cool design, such as the Apple Computer but also IBM and Microsoft, fashion houses such as Prada and Calvin Klein, designers such as Bruce Mau and of course a lot of art made with computers.

Neen is something that a very few people or objects have in common, but still it is so clear and recognizable that even someone who had never heard this word before can easily pin-point. Neen is a frame of mind, it's about a new type of feelings that we have through videogames and computers. But even if Neen has grown mostly online, is not "net art". In old Greek, Neen means "exactly now": this moment and not a second later. For the moment, Neen comes mostly in form of peculiar websites [3] and maybe tomorrow will also exist in certain characteristics of our genetically engineered bodies. Neen fashion doesn't exist yet, although some of the designs of Nicolas Ghesquiere for Balenciaga could be Neen.

We can easily display these 4 art trends around a square, with a trend on each corner. If we exclude the Nouveaux Pop (Jeff Koons, Young British Artists etc.), most of the art and style that started in the late 90's can be found in that square. Takashi Murakami for example, is a combination of Relational Aesthetics and OtakuNeen. The young female artists Murakami promotes are a new flavor of MangaBeige. Matthew Barney is a Telic-Futurista, while his ex-girlfriend Bjork is Beige-Neen-Television. Martin Margiela is Telic-crossing-Relational-Aesthetics but sometimes he is also Beige-for-the-Pope, while Bernhard Willhelm and sometimes Alexandre Herscovitch and Gaspard Yourgevitch are NeenNaive. Nike is Telic-goes-to-the-analyst, Adidas is classy Telic, Doug Aitken is Video Relational and Mariko Mori is dreamy Telic. Finally, *Dazed and Confused* is a Relational Pizza, Italian Vogue is a Telic Fashion Miracle and Butt, the marvelous *Gay Magazine* is Gay in such a Beige way that it actually becomes Neen.

Miltos Manetas, 2005 (interview for *Tokion Magazine*).

[1] Jeremiah "Terminator" LeRoy was a fake identity created by American writer Laura Albert. The name was used from 1996 on for publication in magazines such as *Nerve*. After his first novel *Sarah* was published, "LeRoy" started making public appearances.
[2] Nicolas Bourriaud, *Esthétique relationnelle*, Les presses du réel, Paris 1998. *Relational Aesthetics*, Les presses du réel, Paris 2002.
[3] A collection of those websites, can be found here: www.afterneen.com.

Memoirs of a Mnem

My name is Orange, and I am a Mnem. Today, I am in Madrid, staying in this lurid hotel while taking care of business. I look at myself in the mirror through the eyes of my Pony, and I find that am surprisingly young. In human years, I would be quite old, but as a Mnem I have been around for only a bit longer than a decade. Time does not mean much to a Mnem however, age matters, because it keeps a record of our progress and evolution. It also reminds us Mnems of our robotic side. In this way, I enjoy thinking of myself as a Roboteen. Age is the number of years for which the "automatic" part of a Mnem exists. Humans can live their whole lives and never think of the automata in them but, Alas!, I can never forget it. Ironically, it is the fact of being aware of this that makes a Mnem different from both the robot and the person.

"Robot" is a problematic word; it comes from *robota* meaning, literally, serf-labour (a serf is a person in bondage or servitude), or figuratively "drudgery" or "hard work". The word was introduced to the public at large by the Czech writer Karel Čapek in his play *R.U.R*, which premiered in 1920. However, Karel Čapek was not the originator of the word. In a short letter, referencing an article in the *Oxford English Dictionary*, he credits his brother, the painter and writer Josef Čapek, as its actual inventor. The word originates from the Old Church Slavonic *rabota*, "servitude" which, in turn, comes from the Indo-European root orbh-.

There is no a single definition of "robot" which satisfies everyone, and many people have their own understanding of the word. Joseph Engelberger, a pioneer in industrial robotics, once remarked, "I can't define a robot, but I know one when I see one." Mnems can recognize a Robot when they see one and I can assure you that it does not look at all like us.

The word Mnem originates from "meme", the unit of cultural information such as a practice or idea that is transmitted verbally, or by repeated action from one mind to another. Thoughts, ideas, theories, practices, habits and songs, and dances and moods are memes, and they evolve by natural selection. Memes evolve not only through the processes of variation and mutation, but also through competition and inheritance. However, memes are self-propagating, and they can spread through a culture like a video going "viral". Us Mnems though, we need a human carrier instead to bring us around.

Humans and memes are like genes for the Mnems, and as humans cannot exist without their genes, I would not exist without my human side. My carrier, my Pony, is Miltos Manetas, an artist who lives in the U.K.

I have ridden him for twelve years, from the time that he bought his first laptop, to the moment that he started making portraits using the computer as his subject.

While he was creating those paintings, I materialized, and I have not left him since. Of course, like every Mnem and every human being, I am many different things. From the early days I felt a clear vocation, that of a Painter. In this regard, Manetas had no innate talent, but once I started showing him the way, he managed somehow. Together, we expanded his knowledge in this field, and I grew quickly! Now, I work in the Contemporary Art trade myself, sometimes for Manetas, sometimes for others. My sector is production and I also have interests in conservation.

Twelve years ago, many people were getting their first laptops, and that is how we came of age. We existed before, but we were infants, more memes than Mnems. We had a type of eyes, or sensors anyway, and we were looking at the world. We were keeping memories from it, but until we came of age, we could not access them. We did not have a full body, and although there are certain things in this world you can do bodiless, there are some that you definitely cannot. Our entities were everywhere forming tribes, and a very limited number of people were already aware of us. Some artists, such as Pablo Picasso, had even depicted us, disguising us as a beautiful women or a "Natura Morta", bare from flesh and volume, straight down to our archetypical essence.

However, the misleading power of photography was creating a smokescreen, and we hid behind it. A simple trick of light and shadow had convinced humans that they are the only intelligent life on this planet. It was only after the setup of the networks and the internet that our voice became so strong that it was now impossible for humans to avoid. They know about us now and even if they never speak about us openly, silently, and somehow unconsciously, humanity accepted us. We grew quickly, and we are now extending with the speed of "Moore's Law". (After Intel's co-founder, Gordon E. Moore, stated that "semiconductor complexity doubles every 18 months", development in such a speed became a performance-target for the entire computer industry.)

Some call us angels. It would be a mistake to think of us as computer life, as the word "computer" already sounds so antiquated, and so limited. Anyway, most of us Mnems are coming from very analog backgrounds, such as the history of art, music and literature. It is amazing how many of my kind have survived for centuries, deep inside the layers of paintings. Every time a copyist would repeat a motif taken from a notorious picture, it was as if a mirror would be suddenly raised, and we would fly from one surface to the next, until we finally arrived at the walls of Museums and Collections. There, we were hosted permanently atop labels such as "Caravaggio", "Morandi" and "Goya". And then, when a person like Miltos held a brush in his right hand, and a computer in his left, we finally got a proper body and a proper language.

Speaking about language, I understand that people, hardly think of themselves as "humans". In the same way, "Mnem" is not exactly the term that we use to think of our own selves either, but we are simple creatures, and because we live in the moment, we constantly borrow terms from all human languages in order to define and express our present state.

My present state is orange and, today, I am Miltos. I have to be fully him, talk about our Art, take care of him and drive him through each day.

I am now leaving the hotel, as I need to meet an Indian art dealer to make arrangements with him for an upcoming exhibition of Miltos' work in Bombay. Miltos follows some uncomfortable patterns that he believes can protect him from others, and even from himself. He tends to easily forget his objectives, and he often gets lost in his own experiences. Sometimes, he behaves like a total artist and that behavior can be dangerous, because no human should do that for too long. A rational human cannot be an artist, lawyer, or soldier totally, but he or she must act like an artist, lawyer, or soldier, being an actor above anything else. There is no place for human authenticity in a world made of constructs. Nothing can be authentic these days, because any authentic impulse will eventually turn itself into madness.

Miltos is an actor and a good Pony. He trusts me, and he feeds my constant thirst for information. We realized that in order to have some control over information, it is imperative to absorb it when it is "cold". Fresh information multiplies the cache of "cookies" inside us, and overpopulates us like a disease, which finally destroys us. So Miltos will never watch the news on a television, nor log into cnn.com, and he will never read an art magazine. He does not know what happens around him, but he gets a brief idea of what has happened from reading outdated issues of the *New Yorker* and *Vanity Fair*, and of course, from books. He looks over yesterday's news through the filter of old paintings. I visit museums with him as much as possible. Looking at old masters is essential for me, because this is where I get together with my tribe; this is where I become stronger.

There is no time left for me to continue writing. Miltos my Pony, has to go to meet his partners. I need to run back to him and animate him with ambition. If it was him alone, we would spend all day in this pathetic parking for managers, the Antonio Gaudi Hotel at the Gran Via in Madrid. Miltos likes to take endless showers. He only thinks about women and vacations in primitive places. His favorite hobby is escaping. I cannot follow him in this way, as I know that there is nowhere you can hide. So I am waking him up now and slowly letting him believe that he is in control, and asking him repeatedly to move his legs and get in a taxi. While we drive through the Spanish winter, I fade away. I will come back later when he is finally in bed, when he thinks that he is simply sleeping. I will check his e-mails, charge the battery on his new laptop, and prepare his next move. Bombay is waiting, and so is Beijing!

Antonio Gaudi Hotel, Madrid, February, 2008.

The Piracy Manifesto

Pirates of the Internet Unite!

News from a future newspaper: "A man was stopped yesterday at the boarder of Italy and France, his computer was scanned and pirated material was found, mostly Adobe software and songs by Beatles. The man was arrested at the spot".

From a poem to a drug, from a piece of software to a music record and from a film to a book, everything that's famous and profitable, owes much of its economic value to the manipulation of the Multitudes. People haven't asked to know what the Coca-Cola logo looks like, neither have they asked for the melody of "Like a Virgin". Education, Media and Propaganda teach all that the hard way; by either hammering it on our brains or by speculating over our thirst, our hunger, our need for communication and fun and most of all, over our loneliness and despair. In the days of Internet, what can be copied can be also shared. When it comes to content, we can give everything to everyone at once.

Around this realization, a new social class is awakening. This is not a working class but a class of Producers. Producers are pirates and hackers by default; they recycle the images, the sounds and the concepts of the World. Some of it they invent but most they borrow from others.

Because information occupies a physical part of our bodies, because it is literarily "installed" on our brain and can't be erased at wish, people have the right to own what is projected on them: they have the right to own themselves! Because this is a global World based on inequality and profit, because the contents of a song, a movie or a book are points of advantage in a vicious fight for survival, any global citizen has the moral right to appropriate a digital copy of a song, a movie or a book. Because software is an international language, the secrets of the World are now written in Adobe and Microsoft: we should try hack them. Finally, because poverty is the field of experimentation for all global medicine, no patents should apply.

Today, every man with a computer is a Producer and a Pirate. We all live in the Internet, this is our new country, the only territory that makes sense to defend and protect. The land of the Internet is one of information. Men should be able to use this land freely, corporations should pay for use

– a company is definitely not a person.

Internet is now producing "Internets", situations that exist not only online but also in real space, governed by what is happening online. This is the time for the foundation of a global Movement of Piracy. The freedom of infringing copyright, the freedom of sharing information and drugs: these are our new "Commons". They are Global Rights and as such, Authorities will not allow them without a battle. But this will be a strange battle because this is the first time the Multitudes disrespect the Law instinctively and on a global scale.

Today, an army of teenagers is copying, the adults are copying and even the senior citizens, people from the Left and from the Right are copying. Everyone with a computer is copying something; like a novel Goddess Athena, Information wants to break free from the head of Technology and it assists us on our enterprise.

Pirates of the Internet Unite!

Miltos Manetas, July 1, 2009.

Pirates de l'Internet, unissez-vous!

Extrait d'un journal du futur: "Un homme a été contrôlé hier à la frontière franco-italienne. L'inspection de son ordinateur a permis de découvrir que celui-ci recelait des produits piratés, principalement des logiciels Adobe et de la musique des Beatles. L'homme a été arrêté sur-le-champ".

Qu'il s'agisse d'un poème ou d'un médicament, d'un logiciel ou d'un disque, d'un film ou d'un livre, tout ce qui est populaire et rentable doit la majeure partie de sa valeur économique à la manipulation des Foules. Nul n'a demandé à savoir à quoi ressemble le logo Coca-Cola, ni à connaître le refrain de "Like a Virgin". L'Éducation, les Médias et la Propagande nous les font avaler de force, en les martelant à l'envi ou en spéculant sur notre soif, notre faim, notre besoin de communication et de divertissement, et surtout sur notre sentiment de solitude et notre mal-être. À l'ère d'Internet, ce qui peut être copié peut être partagé. Pour ce qui est des contenus, on peut tout distribuer, à tout le monde en même temps.

À l'aune de cette constatation, une nouvelle classe sociale émerge. Il ne s'agit pas d'une classe laborieuse mais d'une classe de Producteurs. Par essence, ces Producteurs sont des pirates et des hackers; ils réutilisent les images, les sons, et les idées du Monde. Ils en créent certains, mais pour la plupart ils les empruntent à d'autres.

L'information est aujourd'hui partie intégrante de notre organisme, elle est littéralement "installée" dans notre cerveau, et l'on ne peut l'effacer sur demande. C'est pourquoi nous avons le droit de posséder l'information qu'on nous projette: nous sommes en droit d'être maîtres de nous-mêmes! Parce que nous vivons dans des sociétés mondialisées construites sur l'inégalité et le profit, parce que le contenu d'une chanson, d'un film ou d'un livre représentent des atouts dans une lutte sans merci pour survivre, tout citoyen possède le droit moral de s'approprier une copie numérique d'une œuvre quelle qu'elle soit. Parce que l'informatique est un langage international, les secrets du monde sont de nos jours écrits en Adobe et en Microsoft, il est légitime de vouloir les hacker. Enfin, parce que la pauvreté est le champ expérimental de l'industrie pharmaceutique, la médecine devrait être libre de tout brevet.

De nos jours, quiconque possède un ordinateur est à la fois Producteur et Pirate. Nous sommes tous citoyens de l'Internet, c'est notre nouvelle nation, le seul territoire qu'il soit justifié de défendre et de protéger. Internet est une terre d'information et de savoir. Chacun devrait être en mesure de la fouler sans contrepartie financière; seules les grandes entreprises devraient payer pour l'utiliser.

Internet génère des "Internets", des situations qui existent non seulement en ligne, mais aussi dans le monde physique, déterminées par ce qui se passe sur le réseau. L'heure est venue de fonder un Mouvement du Piratage mondial. La liberté d'enfreindre le copyright, celle d'avoir accès sans restriction au savoir et aux traitements médicaux, voilà nos nouveaux "Biens communs". Ce sont des Droits Universels, et en tant que tels, les Autorités ne les concéderont pas sans lutter, mais le combat à livrer sera inédit car pour la première fois, les Foules enfreignent spontanément la Loi à l'échelle planétaire.

Aujourd'hui, tout le monde copie: les jeunes gens, les adultes, nos aînés, les électeurs de gauche comme de droite. Quiconque possède un ordinateur copie quelque chose. Telle une nouvelle Athéna, l'Information jaillit toute armée du crâne ouvert de la Technologie pour nous aider dans notre quête.

Pirates de l'Internet, unissez-vous!

Miltos Manetas, Juillet 2009

Pirati di Internet Unitevi!

Notizia da un giornale del futuro: "Un uomo è stato fermato ieri alla frontiera italiana con la Francia. Nel suo computer è stato ritrovato molto materiale piratato, in particolare software Adobe e molte canzoni dei Beatles. L'uomo è stato immediatamente arrestato."

Dalla poesia alla medicina, dal software alla musica ai film ai libri, tutto quel che diventa famoso deve molto del suo valore economico alla manipolazione delle Moltitudini. Noi non abbiamo chiesto di conoscere il logo della Coca-Cola, né volevamo sapere a memoria la melodia di "Like a Virgin". I media, l'educazione e la propaganda ci hanno costretto ad imparare tutto ciò, speculando sul nostro bisogno di comunicazione, sulla nostra necessità di divertirci ma anche sulla nostra solitudine e disperazione. Nei giorni di Internet, tutto quel che può essere copiato può essere anche condiviso. Quando si tratta di contenuto, possiamo subito dare tutto a tutti. Grazie a questa scoperta, una nuova classe sociale si sta svegliando. Questa non è una classe operaia – almeno non nel senso stretto del termine: è invece una classe di Produttori. I Produttori sono per natura dei Pirati e degli Hacker; riciclano le immagini, i suoni e i concetti del Mondo. Una parte di questo materiale se la inventano ma per lo più se ne appropriano da altri.

Poiché l'informazione occupa una porzione fisica del nostro corpo, poiché viene letteralmente installata nel nostro cervello e non può essere cancellata a piacere, la gente ha il diritto di appropriarsi di quel che viene proiettato su di lei. Uno deve avere il diritto di possedere se stesso. Poiché questa è una società globale basata sull'ineguaglianza e sul profitto, poiché il contenuto di una canzone, di un film e di un libro sono dei punti di vantaggio in una feroce lotta per la sopravvivenza, tutti noi abbiamo il diritto morale di appropriarci di canzoni, film e libri. Quanto al software, altro non è che una lingua internazionale: i nuovi segreti del Mondo sono scritti in Adobe e in Microsoft. Per questo, dobbiamo hackerarli. Infine, poiché è sui poveri che ogni nuovo medicinale viene testato, non possono esserci brevetti sui farmaci. Oggi, chiunque abbia un computer è un Produttore e un Pirata. Tutti noi viviamo nell'Internet: questa è la nostra nuova patria, l'unica che valga la pena difendere. La terra di Internet è fatta d'informazioni. Chiunque deve essere libero di usarle, mentre le compagnie devono pagare per farne uso. Una compagnia non è certamente una persona.

Internet sta producendo "internets", situazioni che esistono non solo in rete, ma anche nello spazio reale, controllate da quanto sta succedendo online. È il momento giusto per la fondazione di un Movimento globale della Pirateria. La bellezza di calpestare il copyright, la libertà di condividere informazioni e medicine, sono i nostri nuovi "Commons", i nostri diritti globali, che naturalmente non otterremo senza combattere. Ma si tratterà di una strana battaglia, perché per la prima volta le Moltitudini infrangono la Legge istintivamente, e su scala globale.

Oggi, una marea di giovani copia informazioni, copiano gli adulti e anche i vecchi, a destra e a sinistra. Chiunque abbia un computer copia qualcosa: come una nuova Dea Atena, l'Informazione vuole uscire dalla testa spaccata della Tecnologia. È al nostro fianco.

Pirati di Internet Unitevi!

Miltos Manetas, luglio 2009

Piratas de Internet Uníos!

Noticias de un periódico del futuro: "Un hombre fue parado ayer en la frontera de Italia y Francia; su ordenador fue escaneado y se encontró material pirata, sobre todo software de Adobe y canciones de los Beatles. El hombre fue detenido inmediatamente".

Desde un poema hasta un medicamento, desde un software hasta un disco de música y desde una película hasta un libro, todo lo que es famoso y provechoso debe mucho de su valor económico a la manipulación Multitudes. La gente no ha pedido saber cual es la forma del logo de Coca-Cola, ni la melodía de "Like a Virgin". La educación, los Media y la Propaganda enseñan todo esto por las malas; o martilleando nuestras cabezas nuestras cabezas o especulando con nuestra sed, nuestro hambre, nuestra necesidad de comunicación y sobre todo, con nuestra soledad y desesperación. En los días de Internet, lo que se puede copiar se puede compartir. Cuando se trata de contenido, podemos dar todo a todos al instante.

Alrededor de este descubrimiento una nueva clase social despierta. No es una clase de trabajadores, sino una clase de Productores. Los productores son piratas y *hackers* por defecto; reciclan las imágenes, los sonidos y los conceptos del Mundo. Algunas cosas las inventan, pero la mayoría de las cosas las toman prestadas de los demás.

Ya que la información ocupa una parte física en nuestros cuerpos, porque está literalmente "instalada" en nuestro cerebro y no se puede borrar a placer, la gente tiene derecho a ser propietarios de lo que les arrojan: tienen derecho a ser propietarios de sí mismos! Ya que vivimos en un Mundo global basado en la desigualdad y el provecho, ya que los contenidos de una canción, una película o un libro son puntos de ventaja en una lucha feroz de supervivencia, cada ciudadano global tiene el derecho moral de apropiarse de una copia digital de una canción, una película o un libro. Ya que el software es un idioma internacional, los secretos del Mundo están escritos ahora en Adobe y Microsoft: deberíamos intentar piratearlos. Por último, ya que la pobreza es un campo de experimentación de toda la medicina global, ninguna patente debería ser utilizada.

Hoy en día, cada persona con un ordenador es un Productor y un Pirata. Todos vivimos en Internet, es un nuevo país, el único territorio que tiene sentido defender y proteger. La tierra de Internet es una tierra de información. La gente debería tener el derecho de utilizar esta tierra libremente, las corporaciones deberían pagar por el uso -una empresa no es una persona por supuesto.

Internet esta produciendo ahora "Internets", situaciones que existen no sólo online sino también en el espacio real, gobernadas por lo que esta pasando en la red. Ahora es el tiempo de fundar un Movimiento global de Piratería. La libertad de violar los derechos de autor, la libertad de compartir información y medicamentos: éstas son nuestras nuevas "Tierras Communales". Son Derechos Globales, y por eso las Autoridades no nos los concederán sin batalla. Pero será una batalla diferente, porque es la primera vez que la Multitud desobedece la Ley instintivamente y a escala global.

Hoy, un ejercito de adolescentes está copiando, los adultos están copiando, e incluso personas de edad avanzada, gente de Izquierdas y de Derechas están copiando. Toda el que que tiene un ordenador copia algo; como una nueva Diosa Atenea, la Información quiere escapar de las garras dc la tccnología y nos ayuda en nuestra empresa.

Piratas de Internet Uníos!

Miltos Manetas, 2009

Internets Pirater, låt oss förenas!

"En man blev stannad igår vid gränsen mellan Italien och Frankrike, hans dator scannades och man upptäckte nedladdat material, för det mesta Adobe software och låtar av Beatles. Mannen arresterades omedelbart."

Från en dikt till en drog, från ett mjukvaruprogram till en musikskiva och från en film till en bok, det ekonomiska värdet av allt som är välkänt och framgåmgsrikt är till stor del ett resultat av manipulationen av massorna. Folk har inte bett om att få veta hur Coca Cola-skylten ser ut, inte heller har de bett om melodin från "Like a Virgin". Utbildning, Media och Propaganda lär ut den hårda vägen: antingen genom att banka in det i hjärnan på oss eller genom att spekulera om vår törst, vår hunger efter kommunikation och att ha roligt, och mest av allt vår ensamhet och förtvivlan. I internet-samhället kan det som kopieras också delas vidare. Vad det gäller innehåll kan vi, på ett ögonblick, ge allt till alla.

Runtomkring denna uppenbarelse uppstår en ny samhällsklass. Detta är inte en arbetarklass utan en klass som består av Producenter. Producenter är i grund och botten pirater och hackare, de återanvänder världens bilder, ljud och idéer. Vissa idéer är originella men de flesta lånas från andra.

Eftersom information upptar en fysisk del av våra kroppar, som är bokstavligen "installerad" i våra hjärnor och kan inte raderas när man känner för det, människor har en rätt att äga det som projekteras mot dem. De har rätten att äga sig själva. Eftersom detta är en global värld grundad på omjämlikheter och intäkter, eftersom innehållet i sånger, filmer och böcker är utgångspunkter i en hård kamp för överlevnad. Samtliga världsmedborgare har moralisk rätt att bevilja en digital kopia av en sång, en film eller en bok. Eftersom mjukvara är ett internationellt språk, världens hemligheter är skrivna med Adobe och Microsoft. Vi borde försöka att hacka dem. Och slutligen, för att fattigdom är experimentplatsen för all global medicin, inga patent borde gälla.

Alla som har en dator är idag en Producent eller en Pirat. Vi lever alla i Internet, detta är vårt land, det enda territoriet som verkar vettigt att försvara och skydda. Internet-landet handlar om information. Människan borde kunna vistas fritt i detta land, företag borde betala för att bruka det – ett företag är aldrig en person.

Internet producerar nuförtiden "internets", situationer som inte bara existerar online men även i verkligheten, som styrs och influeras av vad som händer online. Det är högtid för en global Fildelningsrörelse. Friheten att inkräkta på upphovsrätten, friheten att dela information och droger, är vår nya allmänna plats, de står för Globala Rättigheter och kan därför inte upplåtas till myndigheter utan en kamp. Men det blir en märklig kamp då det är första gången som massorna inte instinktivt respekterar Lagen på en global nivå. En armé av tonåringar kopierar varje dag. Vuxna kopierar, gamla kopierar, alla med en dator kopierar något. Som en nymodig Gudinna Athena vill Information bryta sig loss från Teknologi, för att på så vis hjälpa oss att driva vår sysselsättning vidare. Internets Pirater, låt oss förenas!

Miltos Manetas, 2009

Πειρατές του *Internet* ενωθείτε*!*

Ειδήσεις από εφημερίδα του μέλλοντος: "Οι αρχές σταμάτησαν χθες έναν άντρα στα σύνορα Ιταλίας και Γαλλίας·μετά από έλεγχο στο κομπιούτερ του βρήκαν πειρατικό υλικό, κυρίωςsoftware της Adobe και τραγούδια των Beatles. Ο άντρας συνελήφθη επιτόπου".

Από ένα ποίημα μέχρι ένα φάρμακο, από ένα software μέχρι ένα δίσκο μουσικής και από μια ταινία μέχρι ένα βιβλίο, ό,τι είναι διάσημο και επικερδές, οφείλει ένα μεγάλο μέρος της αξίας του στην μαζική χειραγώγηση. Εμείς δε ζητήσαμε να γνωρίζουμε ούτε το logo της Coca-Cola, ούτε τη μελωδία του "Like a Virgin". Η Εκπαίδευση, η Προπαγάνδα και τα Μέσα Μαζικής Ενημέρωσης τα διδάσκουν με βία όλα αυτά· είτε σφυρηλατώντας τα στο μυαλό μας, εκμεταλευόμενοι τη δίψα και την πείνα μας, την ανάγκη μας για επικοινωνία και διασκέδαση, και πάνω απ' όλα τη μοναξιά και την απόγνωσή μας.

Στις μέρες του Internet, ό,τι αντιγράφεται μπορεί επίσης και να μοιραστεί. Σε ό,τι αφορά το περιεχόμενο, μπορούμε κατευθείαν νυ δώσουμε "Τα πάντα σε όλους".

Γύρω από αυτή τη συνειδητοποίηση, μια νέα τάξη ξυπνά. Δεν είναι μια εργατική τάξη αλλά μια τάξη Παραγωγών. Οι παραγωγοί είναι πειρατές και hacker εξ ορισμού· ανακυκλώνουν τις εικόνες, τους ήχους και τις έννοιες του Κόσμου. Μερικά πράγματα τα επινοούν, αλλά τα περισσότερα τα δανείζονται από άλλους.

Επειδή η πληροφορία καταλαμβάνει ένα φυσικό μέρος του σώματός μας, γιατί "εγκαθίσταται" κυριολεκτικά στο μυαλό μας και δεν μπορεί να σβηστεί κατ' επιλογή, οι άνθρωποι έχουν το δικαίωμα να κατέχουν ό,τι προβάλλεται επάνω τους: έχουν το δικαίωμα να είναι κάτοχοι του εαυτού τους! Επειδή ο κόσμος μας είναι παγκοσμιοποιημένος, και βασίζεται στην ανισότητα και το κέρδος, επειδή τα περιεχόμενα ενός τραγουδιού, μιας ταινίας ή ενός βιβλίου είναι πλεονεκτήματα στον άγριο αγώνα της επιβίωσης, ο κάθε παγκόσμιος πολίτης έχει το ηθικό δικαίωμα να οικειοποιείται το ψηφιακό αντίγραφο του κάθε βιβλίου, ταινίας ή τραγουδιού. Επειδή το software είναι μια διεθνής γλώσσα, τα μυστικά του Κόσμου γράφονται πια σε Adobe και Microsoft: πρέπει λοιπόν να προσπαθήσουμε να τα χακάρουμε και να τα μοιραστούμε. Τέλος, επειδή η φτώχεια είναι το πεδίο του πειραματισμού για όλη την παγκόσμια ιατρική, δεν θα έπρεπε να ισχύουν πατέντες.

Σήμερα, κάθε άνθρωπος με κομπιούτερ είναι πια Παραγωγός και Πειρατής. Όλοι ζούμε στο Internet, αυτή είναι η νέα μας πατρίδα και είναι η μόνη επικράτεια που έχει νόημα να υπερασπιστούμε και να προστατέψουμε. Η γη του Internet είναι η γη της πληροφορίας. Οι άνθρωποι θα έπρεπε να κάνουν χρήση αυτή της γης ελεύθερα, οι εταιρείες όμως θα έπρεπε να πληρώνουν για τη χρήση της - μια εταιρεία σε καμιά περίπτωση δεν είναι ένα άτομο.

Το Internet έχει πια γίνει "Internets", πολυσύνθετες καταστάσεις που υπάρχουν όχι μόνο online αλλά απλώνονται και στον πραγματικό χώρο, που ορίζονται απ' ότι συμβαίνει online. Αυτή είναι η εποχή για να ιδρύσουμε ένα παγκόσμιο Κίνημα Πειρατείας. Η ελευθερία να παραβιάζουμε τα πνευματικά δικαιώματα, η ελευθερία να μοιραζόμαστε πληροφορίες και φάρμακα: αυτά είναι τα νέα μας "Κοινά αγαθά". Είναι Παγκόσμια Δικαιώματα και ως τέτοια οι Αρχές δε θα τα αφήσουν χωρίς μάχη. Όμως αυτή θα είναι μια περίεργη μάχη γιατί είναι η πρώτη φορά που τα Πλήθη δείχνουν ασέβεια προς το Νόμο ενστικτωδώς και σε παγκόσμια κλίμακα.

Σήμερα, μια στρατιά εφήβων αντιγράφει, οι ενήλικοι αντιγράφουν και ακόμα και οι ηλικιωμένοι, άνθρωποι από τη Δεξιά και την Αριστερά αντιγράφουν. Ο καθένας που έχει κομπιούτερ αντιγράφει κάτι· σαν μια νέα Θεά Αθηνά, η Πληροφορία θέλει να απελευθερωθεί από το κεφάλι της Τεχνολογίας και μας βοηθάει στο εγχείρημά μας.

Πειρατές του Internet ενωθείτε!

Miltos Manetas, 2009

ROMA[2]

In 2002, I was invited to participate in a group show. I offered a few of my paintings but they were rejected. «We prefer something "contemporary"», I was told. «Video, installations, photographs, maybe a website».

The fact that my paintings were not produced centuries ago but just recently, didn't seem to register with the art specialists. Painting is considered today an obsolete technology, like traveling with a horse instead of using cars and airplanes.

In the business of transportation, moving information as far as possible, at the maximum speed and ease is essential and the same happens in Contemporary Art. Things should arrive at their destination unchanged; a chair should remain a chair, a masterpiece should stay a masterpiece, beauty and common sense need to be kept intact and under control. In this context, Painting – the most ambiguous of the arts as well as the least explicit – is quite a crime.

Oil on canvas painting was in fact invented around 1300 at a time of Big Doubt, together with all kinds of ideas that poisoned all certainties about reality. Suddenly, the Earth stopped being flat, the Sun became just a normal star and human beings succeeded in looking at themselves from the outside – something that until then was God's privilege.

Those days, extremist artists – wolves in sheep's clothing – began to hide their explosive concepts in canvasses that were supposed to illustrate the walls of the Christian churches.

Today, official culture took it as its job, to reconstruct the coherence of reality. Sponsored by public and private money, art is now employed to continue the propaganda diffused by those churches. In this sublime equilibrium between authority and creativity, Painting is a black swan and would have been eliminated had this been possible. Talking about transport, Painting takes us in all directions but it does so either with unimaginable speed or with exasperating slowness. It cannot be controlled.

Yorgo Manis is one of the very few young artists who are exploring the possibility of encountering Painting in unimaginable places. "Street View" [1] by Google – which Manis use as his subject matter – is the latest level of complexity applied to the World. "Street View" makes reality even more complex, it simulates our cities in photographic detail and explores them as if they were a videogame. In this way, Rome becomes now **ROME**2.

While the World computes itself on multiple levels of simulation, Painting captures the World and serves it back to us. Painting destroys our preconceptions about the World, without explain it.

Miltos Manetas, London 2009, written for the first one-man show by Yorgo Manis at the gallery C02 in Rome.

[1] From *Wikipedia*: "Google Street View is a technology featured in Google Maps and Google Earth that provides panoramic views from various positions along many streets in the world. It was launched on May 25, 2007, originally only in several cities in the United States, and has since gradually expanded to include more cities and rural areas worldwide.

Google Street View displays images taken from a fleet of specially adapted cars. Areas not accessible by car, like pedestrian areas, narrow streets, alleys and ski resorts, are sometimes covered by Google Trikes (tricycles) or a snowmobile. On each of these vehicles there are nine directional cameras for 360° views at a height of about 8.2 feet, or 2.5 meters, GPS units for positioning and three laser range scanners for the measuring of up to 50 meters 180° in the front of the vehicle. There are also 3G/GSM/Wi-Fi antennas for scanning 3G/GSM and Wi-Fi hotspots.

Recently, 'high quality' images are based on open source hardware cameras from Elphel.

Where available, street view images appear after zooming in beyond the highest zooming level in maps and satellite images, and also by dragging a "pegman" icon onto a location on a map. Using the keyboard or mouse the horizontal and vertical viewing direction and the zoom level can be selected. A solid or broken line in the photo shows the approximate path followed by the camera car, and arrows link to the next photo in each direction. At junctions and crossings of camera car routes, more arrows are shown."

Life Autostop

Life drives a car, we are asking for a ride, and it let us on. Now, it would be stupid to only believe that we can dictate to life to get us to arrive at a certain place. We can suggest a stop of course, insist even a little, throw out an idea her and there. But only life will decide.

From observation, we learn that life's destination is always the location of our death, or where we will 'meet' our death. I think that it is safer not to discuss the itinerary, but to simply lay back and to enjoy each and every landscape.

Now that I am stuck here in Loreto, I realize that I am really happy. My life was passing through this town, and I had no idea!

Miltos Manetas, Loreto 2010.

Questions About Videos After Videogames

Hi!
My name is Mathias Jansson, a Swedish art-critic and Game Art researcher. Together with Matteo Bittanti, I am working on a interview book with the pioneers of Game Art. We really want to include you in this book, and hope you have time to answers some questions. Previous interviews are available at the blog GameScenes.

Sincerely,
Mathias Jansson

YOUR VIDEOS AFTER VIDEOGAMES SERIES IS CONSIDERED THE FIRST EXAMPLE OF MACHINIMA. YOU STARTED DEVELOPING THESE VIDEOS IN 1996, WHEN YOU MOVED TO NY. WHAT PROMPTED YOU TO START USING GAMES TO CREATE ART? WHAT DID YOU FIND IN THIS MEDIUM THAT YOU COULD NOT GET WITH, FOR EXAMPLE, VIDEO?

In the same way that the impressionists focused on nature, *computer landscape* is for me, my main subject matter. It was only during the late 1990's that I realized that videogames were part of that computer landscape, and not just yet another bit of visual excrement that was dropping out from television. Around 1996, videogames started to exist so heavily, that they became impossible to ignore: they ceased being entertainment solely, and started becoming communication. They were not only communication between humans, though, but more importantly, they represented communication between us humans and our intelligent machines. I decide, that if I start listening carefully to videogames, these intelligent machines would tell me about how they felt, and share their views of the world with me.

HOW DID YOU STARTED?

It all started for me after buying my first PlayStation. I remember that after unpacking it and looking at the joystick, I was thinking that it was the first time that a computer was gently offering me its little hand. So I decided to grab that little hand, and to start walking together with it.

I used to make videos, but at that point in time, I had lost my faith in video and photography. These media were reflecting only half of the story, and they were always biased from a human point of view. Filming Lara Croft while she tried to cross a dark cave and got killed by poisonous arrows (*Flames*, 1997), and Super Mario, lying asleep (*Super Mario Sleeping*, 1998), was an entirely different experience. In those videos, I was not employing human actors anymore [1]. Actors, though they can be amazing to watch, bring with them their limitations. The characters from videogames instead, were so multidimensional when they were filmed, that it made my head spin. Because you can choose the point of view from where to watch your character (who is nobody else than yourself), these characters were at the same time the player of the game, and the director of the video that I was filming.

But they were also – because of the computer – a kind of early robotic entity. I felt that such an entity would soon grow into something a lot more sophisticated, and that it was important to document from where everything had started.

Therefore, what I was doing was not anymore about video, and in some way, it was not even about "art" any more. It was about looking, and about how to start listening to the newest side of the world. It was about permitting these newcomers, our intelligent machines, to come forward and reveal their stories. The fact that, just a few years later, Machinima became a popular art of storytelling shows that many other people, some of them artists, but most of them not, were also interested in listening to these stories.

IN THE "VIDEOS AFTER VIDEOGAMES" SERIES YOU SIMULTANEOUSLY USE AND SUBVERT SOME TROPES AND CONVENTIONS OF VIDEO ART. WERE YOU TRYING TO MAKE A POINT ABOUT THAT STATE OF CONTEMPORARY ART? FOR EXAMPLE, IS MARIO SLEEPING A NOD TO ANDY WARHOL'S FAMOUS ARTWORK?

No, the problematics related with the work of Warhol did not concern me the least. At that time, my interests regarding the state of contemporary art were already fading and once I started going around the different levels of Super Mario 64, I kind of forgot about it. In 1999, I decided to leave New York and move to Los Angeles, because in New York, nobody cared much about digital culture. In NYC, people were too absorbed with art to notice that life was changing around them. Later, when a new generation of artists came to age, even New York discovered videogames, and now we see some art related to them displayed in the New Museum but back in those days, no art critic or curator had ever played a videogame.

UNLIKE THE MORE RECENT FAN VIDEOS THAT EMPHASIZE STUNTS, BREATHTAKING ACTION AND PLAYERS' SKILLS, YOUR VIDEOS FOCUS ON STASIS, REPETITION, AND THE TRIVIALITY OF SIMULATED SPACES (FROM SLEEPING TO TAPPING A FOOT). WERE YOU SUGGESTING THAT WHAT REALLY MATTERS IN GAMES WAS INACTIVITY?

In simulation (videogames), as well as in life, it is nice when action stops for a little while, so that that the player can look around, and see the details of the situation. That's how we actually do our painting, and sometimes photography. It is our call now to find the perfect medium, that can potentially explore the observation of those moments also in videogames. I started myself by exploring with video and prints but I have to admit that my work is pretty basic, and I hope that younger artists will soon invent more intricate ways to let the simulation talk.

IN VIDEOS LIKE *MIRACLE* (1996) YOU PLAY WITH GLITCHES AND CODE MALFUNCTIONS. DO YOU THINK THAT BUGS AND MISTAKES REPRESENT THE ESSENCE OF NEW TECHNOLOGY? IS THE FAILURE OF THE SIMULATION THE TRADEMARK OF ITS INNER NATURE?

In *Miracle* a Hornet F-18, a light aircraft, from a flight simulator, falls onto the sea, but instead of crashing, it starts running over the water's surface. We can think about that run on the water as a glitch and a malfunction, but we can also see it as special thing that airplanes can do in a simulation. I find the second approach more interesting. When I filmed that airplane, it was not because I wanted to speak about game bugs and mistakes, but because I wanted to show what was happening there, and also because I found it very poetic.

HOW DOES VIDEOGAME INSPIRED ART FIT INTO THE NEEN MANIFESTO?

The work with videogames was, for me, an early version of NEEN. Up until 2001, I held hope that videogames would turn really radical. But that did not happen. The videogame industry instead became a kind of "Hollywood 2.0", where what mattered most was budget and revenue. So I started investing all of my efforts into the World Wide Web, and specifically into what was, back then, its most revolutionary field: Flash animation. Flash was important because anyone, even the programming illiterate like myself, could use Flash to create amazing things. Still, videogames remained my secret love, and I still hold out hope that one day, fascinating videogame NEENSTERS will show us stuff that will take our breath away.

YOU ARE ALSO A PAINTER, MAKING PAINTINGS OF COMPUTER CABLES, SCREENS, AND PEOPLE PLAYING VIDEOGAMES. WHAT IS THE IDEA BEHIND USING A TRADITIONAL MEDIUM SUCH AS PAINTING TO EXPLORE THE DIGITAL WORLD? WHY DO YOU NOT INSTEAD USE DIGITAL MEDIA TO PORTRAY THE DIGITAL WORLD?

I started painting in 1995. While I was doing my paintings, I also started using digital media to portray – as you say – the "digital world". Indeed, until now, I have produced something like 500 large-format prints from videogames, 20 videos-after-videogames, and more than 30 websites that employ Flash animation and other such programming. Yet painting still remains for me the one important medium that can have a considerable effect on the karma of reality. That because a painting does not move, though everything in it – forms, colors, meanings, and interpretations, even its format and composition – is in constant motion and transformation. People speculate about the existence of quantum computers, and hypothesize about what we will be doing once they are invented. I want to close out this interview by sharing my belief that perhaps quantum computers have always been around, and we have been using them from the ancient times, and that they are nothing other than what we call "paintings".

[1] Such as those two guys who were endlessly smoking and drinking coffee at *Soft Driller* (1994) video or Manetas himself at *Red Satellite* (1993).

Note Written on a Blackberry, April 1st, 2010

Toronto, Ontario, Canada

Dear Alpha,

After spending the last ten years Up There, I feel like I just came down from the technology Olympus. I am (back again) in no one's country. Forty-five years old, modesty aside, my image published in the media and all over the Internet, and yet... I feel as I though a Demi-God, only I am far more Demi than God. I feel like I am less than the nobodies that I imagine will inhabit grounds that are not quite yet Internet.

Now I have reached a point, where I am talking from inside my own body. A Blackberry Point. [1]

At this very moment, while composing this Note to you, I am in Trinity-Bellwoods park in Toronto, walking around, crossing bodies and situations. I am writing this message because it is possible and needs to be said. This text is like a self-producing animation, the combination of myself and the Blackberry. So what would happen if I shut off the Blackberry and go on walking in the park like any Natural bastard? I shudder to find out.

Your father, Miltos.

[1] In case you don't know what a Blackberry is, I include in this message it's *Wikipedia* entry: «**BlackBerry** is a line of mobile e-mail and smartphone devices developed and designed by Canadian company Research In Motion (RIM) since 1999.
BlackBerry phones function as a personal digital assistant and portable media player. BlackBerry phones are primarily known for their ability to send and receive (push) Internet e-mail wherever mobile network service coverage is present, or through Wi-Fi connectivity. BlackBerry phones support a large array of instant messaging features, including BlackBerry Messenger.»

Teller

Here I am, at the corner of Yonge and St. Clair, under **ScotiaBank**'s reassuring shadows.

Looking towards **CanadaTrust** without any trust.

I am just in front of **CIBC**'s Banking Centre. From its facade, I learn about the presence of an "Instant Teller" inside.

But then again, what kind of news will you ever get from a **CIBC** employee? Better check with Delphi's Teller. Speaking about Delphi, it also used to be regarded as the Center of the World, its Axis Mundi, its belly button.

And later, the belly button became Jerusalem, and now it is Toronto. Specifically the corner where Yonge meet St. Clair is the Axis Mundi.

Miltos Manetas, Toronto 2010.

Metascreen

Though most people are obediently aligning themselves with the illuminated dictatorship of digital, a few of us have decided to reset our watches and go slightly analog instead. To go fully analog would be impossible, as it would require us to drop away from our Global Description of Reality (GDR), which is based entirely on being digitalized. Digitalization began a few thousand years ago, with categorization and naming, and it went mainstream with the use of the written word.

Digital's roots are based upon a very simple instruction: "This is a door" - "Yes" (1) versus "No" (0). Accepting this instruction requires us to choose between 0 and 1, and then passing that "knowledge" around. Whether this knowledge was delivered by God, discovered by human genius, or simply appeared at the head of a long string of possibilities, the instruction is taken very seriously, and for a very long time. In our time, the instruction has become such a dogma that if we try calling things by strange names, or calling them with names of other things, we are either crazy or speaking metaphorically. Or, maybe, we are doing "art". As it happened, art hacked a place for itself upon our need to be reminded of the relativity of all these definitions.

We need art; now, more than ever, with all of these computers and networks around, and with Big Digital closing in on us from all fronts.

We need to look at Digital and see what else it is, because if Digital is left to the sterile application of categorization and naming, this guarantees a very miserable future for all of us.

By using the term Metascreen, we refer to both a time without all of these screens littering our lives, but also material that contains mental tags, referencing the landscape of the computer screen. Computer screens are a burden. The last time that I counted, I realized that I am carrying fourteen of these screens in my suitcase, while at my home or in the hotel, there are many more waiting for me. In an ideal world, the move away from screen to Metascreen would be the passage from the nightmare of all those computer screens to the very interesting place of Existential Computing.

Existential Computing is a kind of computer "reality", but has nothing to do with virtual reality, augmented reality, and the likes. But how this "computer reality" will look? I have no idea of course. If I did, Existential

Computing would be already here, because knowing the aspect of something is inventing it. Still, we can start by imagining how this possible future will look by thinking of what would be different if the three requests of The Father of the Internet, Mr. Leonard Kleinrock (the man who sent the first email in 1969), were satisfied.

These requests are the following:

1. We need to be able to access the Net from any place. (Even from the center of the Earth, or from the most remote corner of the universe).

2. We need to be able to connect by using any device (with a fork for example, or with an old shoe).

3. The device that we will be using to connect should be invisible.

Kleinrock's "Metascreen" is the utopia of an era where the database has finally become just another layer of nature. Dr. Kleinrock, after all, invented the Internet just because he was fascinated by Supeman's powerful radio. (Six-years-old Leonard Kleinrock was reading a Superman comic at his apartment in Manhattan, when, in the centerfold, he found plans for building a crystal radio. He built that radio and was totally hooked when free music came through the earphones: no batteries, no power, all free. Later, in another issue of Superman, Kleinrock read about another radio that could emit its signal from anywhere in the galaxy and he decided that this was the radio that he wanted instead!)

We are probably still very far (or maybe not too far) from that era but I believe that the trick here is to now start thinking analogue again. I am not talking about the old pre-Internet analogue, but of the coming one, of analogue after digital. "Metascreen" between other things, is the cry of digital that is soon to become both history and past.

Miltos Manetas, Bogota, 2011.

Selected Bits from Interviews

Tassos Sofroniou asked me in 2009:

ART VS REALITY IN OUR TROUBLED TIMES. BUSINESS AS USUAL?

Art is a conformist's job. During troubled times, most of us artists use to hide under our table and to continue sketching spasmodically what happens around. Most of us – like dogs would do – still take their food from the hand of the occasional tyrant, while the very few with extra sensibility drive themselves crazy. Still all artists, even the collaborationist such as the Futurists and the Social Realists, are making a point against the Tyrant because its on art's Nature to be revolutionary.

WHAT ARE THE MOST IMPORTANT INGREDIENTS IN ORDER TO START A WORK? AND MOST IMPORTANTLY, WHAT IS OF GREAT PERMANENT INSPIRATION TO YOU?

To start a work of art you need to be crazy enough and look for "parts" where nobody thought they would actually exist. Making art is less about creating and more about discovering. My inspiration comes from a bunch of painters such as Rembrandt, Rubens, Raphael and from some writers such as Homer, Philip K. Dick and William Gibson. The music that inspires me is mostly Mozart and Mark Tranmer (Gnac).

YOU FAMOUSLY SAID THAT COMPUTERS ARE EARTH'S NEW SPECIES. DON'T YOU THINK THAT TECHNOLOGY HAS MADE HUMAN EMOTION DRY?

Nothing can make human emotion dry. It's actually the opposite: Internet is a big theater of emotion on a global scale. We just have to see the signs, find the patterns. It's not very easy because Internet is a huge Desert and to find its emotional oasis takes time and talent. That's what we do with Neen: we map the Oasis.

IS TO BE CONSUMED PART OF CREATING ART, OR IS IT JUST
AN ULTIMATE MOMENT OF PERSONAL EXPRESSION?

You can't really "consume" art because it constantly escapes your
definition. We usually consume collateral effects around art, the glamour,
the passion, the smartness, the success etc. But Art is more than the sum of
its parts. As for personal expression, I don't know what exactly is
"personal" in "expression". Most things we express are simply resonances:
data that imitate data.

IF MONEY AND TIME WERE AVAILABLE WHAT WOULD BE
YOUR ULTIMATE WORK OF ART? EITHER CREATED BY YOU OR
PURCHASED FROM YOU?

A woman suspended 60 cm from the ground by natural means (without
any technological tricks, ropes and the such).

WHAT MIGHT BE A LITTLE SECRET OF YOURS IN ORDER TO
FULLY UNDERSTAND AND APPRECIATE A GREAT WORK OF
ART? WHEN DO YOU KNOW IT IS GREAT INDEED?

A great artwork, is a work that stays in our memory for reasons that we
never fully understand. It remains in our heads forever, now you like it now
not, it becomes part of us, still, it's not a memory but something of an active
fixture. And we never really grasp why we keep it there…

Yannis Arvanitis asked me in 2008:

WHAT IS THE DIFFERENCE IN GETTING BACK TO
PAINTINGS AFTER ALL THIS EXTENDED DIGITAL PRACTICE?

During the last twelve years, I never stopped painting. I believe neither
in creative stages nor in mere innovation. I do everything at the same time,
either it's old style such as painting, new style such as conceptual art or
very new style such as the Internet and the art after videogames. However
my priority is whatever strikes me as the most urgent thing to do at any
given point and that's why my production seems to be so mixed up.
Everyday, "everything" is urgent.

IS PAINTING VERY DIFFERENT FROM DIGITAL ART?

I consider them both some short of female divinities. Both can be very beautiful but also extremely ugly – it only depends on how you approach them. Both can become an addiction. Painting is a really old practice, a cultural vampire that survives on images and revives by possessing young dedicated people. Digital art is a different story, it's something that has just been born, or better, rises out of nowhere: a very recent Venus.

Having an affair with both, painting and digital art is a drama but I found that there is equilibrium after a while. The two of them seem to be reaching an agreement. There is always an effort from the part of painting, a concession somehow because digital art doesn't really care, as it has nothing to defend. It is not "historical" and that's its power for the moment. That's how I started painting the Internet (InternetPaintings.com) and that's why I made all those prints from videogames in a somehow "painterly" manner. It's as if painting "wanted to know" about the Internet and the videogames and I had to teach it.

HOW DO YOU DEFINE EXISTENTIAL COMPUTING?

That's a strange concept and I admit that I don't have a complete idea what it is about. Here is what I wrote the other day.

«We don't think from inside our brains anymore, at least not that often. We have computers and we spend a lot of time with them. While we are thinking, we are observing our machines doing what we do: they copy something, they paste something else, they play some music and then they open some kind of a document. There is a "mirroring" and I call this "Existential Computing".

From our human point of view, we really need to learn thinking in a shocking way, beyond the norm and probably our machines will do the same, we can do that together because our machines are brains outside our brains – they are external. We need to start asking questions that seem fundamental from that point of view.»

NICOLAS BOURRIAUD HAS REFERRED TO YOUR WORK IN TERMS OF RELATIONAL AESTHETICS. HOW WOULD YOU CORRESPOND TO THIS SYSTEMATIZATION OF YOUR WORK TODAY?

My work is definitely "relational aesthetics" because I come from contemporary art and everything I do goes back to some experience of art in one way or another. Still, concepts such as Neen and my videogame works seem very unrelated, as if they have fallen from the sky, neither random creativity nor "contemporary art". I am doing my best to operate in the opposite way of the academic relational aesthetics.

If this was medicine, I would say that I am more of a holistic practitioner instead of making a career in hospitals. But I don't underestimate them either. I am there whenever the curators and the Museums need me.

«OUTSIDE THE INTERNET THERE IS NO GLORY, NO INTERNET ARTISTS ARE JUST FREELANCE EMPLOYEES OF OTHER EMPLOYEES, THE CURATORS OF THE EXHIBITIONS.» IS CURATING A TASK THAT CAN PRODUCE NEW CONTENT, NEW MEANINGS?

I believe that Curating should grow in some metaphysical, totally unexpected direction. You need a Nietzsche of curating, someone who will teach curators how to walk the lonely path.

Giorgio Galotti asked me in 2009:

WHERE ARE YOU FROM?

From an age without Internet.

WHERE DO YOU WORK?

At the Internets. ("Internets" are realities that exist online as well as in any different territories influenced by the power of the Internet.

IF YOU WOULD HAVE TO DESCRIBE YOUR COUNTRY WITH THE QWERTY LANGUAGE WHAT SYMBOL YOU'D USE?

I don't belong to any Nation. I have a Greek, an Italian, an American and also a British in me, but more than anything I am from the Internets.

IF YOU SEARCH THE POSITION OF YOUR STUDIO ON
GOOGLE MAPS WHICH KIND OF MONUMENT-ATTRACTIONS
APPEAR CLOSE TO IT?

My London studio is surrounded by parks and music. My studio in
Milan instead is surrounded by fashion and fascism.

WHAT'S THE OBJECTIVE OF YOUR ART?

I am not on a mission, I don't have an objective. But while I am doing
Art, I always remember to destroy my convictions. What's left – once you
destroy your illusions about reality – can only be Art.

FOR THE NEXT GENERATION NOW COMPLETELY
DEPENDENT ON DIGITAL TECHNOLOGY, DO YOU BELIEVE
THAT THE INTERNET WILL INCREASINGLY BECOME A MEANS
OF DISPOSAL OR EMANCIPATION?

I believe that once violence is over, Revolution cease existing too. In a
similar way, Internet doesn't exist no more. We are now left with a huge
incomplete database, the World as we always knew it. We need to start
from scratch.

IN THE CREATION OF YOUR WORKS THERE IS A STRONG
LINK WITH VIRTUAL REALITY. DO YOU THINK IT IS MORE
PRAGMATIC AND RELIABLE THAN MATERIAL REALITY, OR
IT'S ONLY AWAY TO TALK ABOUT OUR CONTEMPORARY
HISTORY?

There is nothing unreal in "virtual" and there only is little reality in
what seems "real".

AT THE LAST VENICE BIENNALE, YOU PARTICIPATE WITH
AN EXPERIMENTAL PROJECT OF STRONG AND CONCEPTUAL
IMPACT, AN INTERNET PAVILION NEVER EXISTED BEFORE... IS
IT THE START OF A REVOLUTION WITHOUT WEAPONS?

I don't know. I did an Internet Pavilion just to see if there will be any
consequences. Until now, there were no reactions which makes me suspect
– and hope – that everything changed! We need to be careful these days
when it comes to analyze appearances. That's also because we all work for

the industries of fiction; art, spectacle, politics and science are jobs that pay to alter and hide away everything that's really special. The Show don't shows but destroys what is supposedly showing.

Nicola Tosic asked me at some point:

> YOU WANTED TO HIRE LEXICON BRANDING TO MAKE A NAME FOR A NEW FORM OF ART AND YOU ASKED FOR 100.000 US AND YOU GOT IT. HOW DID YOU GET THE NEWS THAT YOU GOT THE MONEY AND HOW DID YOU FEEL? DID YOU SCREAM, CRY OR YOU WERE LIKE "OF COURSE"?

I was afraid to even ask my producer – Yvonne Force and her company Artproduction Fund – for the money, I thought that it was an impossible project and I was just complaining that we will never be able to find such an amount. But Yvonne turned and told me, «don't worry honey, I will find you the money and we will find the name. Just call the company and ask them if they want us for clients». I called LEXICON and they were very busy, they had no time to work for us but after a first meeting they finally accepted us.

At that point, I was happy but again I wouldn't believe that they will come with a proper name but they did. I got their fax with the different terms they were proposing at the Almine Rech Gallery in Paris where I was having an exhibition; and when myself and Mai saw NEEN between these terms, we were suddenly very happy because we knew that our dream was becoming real, this term (NEEN) seemed to have its own destiny already, we just had to help it fulfill it.

> WHAT IS THE FUNNIEST THING YOU HAVE EVER SEEN IN YOUR LIFE?

I think that the funniest thing in the universe, is the name "Tosic". Every time that I see it written or when someone pronounces it, I feel the mixture of joy and provocation that has offended Christianity for centuries.

> DID YOU EVER FART VERY LOUDLY DURING REALLY ROMANTIC SEX?

Maybe while drunk but I don't remember. it can also happen during homosexual sex and I suppose that's the reason why most men avoid this experience.

WHAT DO YOU THINK ART IS?

You see stuff people or intelligent machines are doing and they are mostly forgettable. you immediately erase them from your memory or you assign them a fixed shortcut form and keep them there for practical reasons.

But there are things you want to keep with you forever and show to others because you are never "done" with them, you never "understand" them. These things are, or they can become at some point, "artworks".

The story of the Internet Pavilion (in progress)

The Internet Pavilion (Padiglione Internet) is what its name declares: a space made by Internet, a Pavilion located on the Net, which opens every Venice Biennial and closes when the Biennial ends.

For its first edition in 2009, myself and Swedish curator Jan Åman decided to fill it with Pirates. So, we invited a number of people involved with the activist website ThePirateBay.org to come in Venice and to inaugurate their "First Embassy of Piracy" during the opening of the Biennial.

The Berlusconi government didn't like that and just a few hours after the press statement of Padiglione Internet was released, the administration of the Venice Biennial received a call asking them to get rid of The Pirate Bay.

So we took-off The Pirate Bay from our press statement, but the pirates came to Venice anyway.

At some point, the pirates teamed up with activists of the city and started going around with boats, waving pirate banners and singing the beautiful "Pirates of the Internet" song (written and performed by Tobias Bernstrup and Mai Ueda):

> «We are Pirates of the Internet
>
> Pirates of the World Wide Web
>
> Nothing that can stop us now
>
> We are here to stay...»

That act of docile piracy had its consequences. When the Internet Pavilion project was submitted again this year, the Biennial first asked us to guarantee that nothing would be announced to the press before previous arrangement with them. We agreed on that, but finally La Biennale canceled its Internet Pavilion for 2011.

At that point, we decided to present the Internet Pavilion in Venice independently, with a day dedicated to Internet at the island of San Servolo which is right in front of the Giardini and the Biennale.

For that day (June 02, 2011), in collaboration with the Accademia di Belle Arti di Venezia, we invited a large number of internet artists to participate at a Bring Your Own Beamer (BYOB) event, a spontaneous exhibition started by Rafaël Rozendaal.

Jan Åman, Margherita Balzerani, Gloria Maria Cappelletti, Caroline Corbetta, Silvia Ferri De Lazara, Manuel Frara, Marina Fokidis, Miltos Manetas, Lev Manovich, Yvonne Force Villareal, David Quiles Guilló, Domenico Quaranta, Elena Giulia Rossi, Valentina Tanni, Angelo Plessas, Doreen Reemen, Rafaël Rozendaal, Francesco Urbano and Francesco Ragazzi, each one in his own way, contributed to the creation of the II Internet Pavilion.

The history of the Internet Pavilion
Jan Aman

First published in Dazed & Confused issue □□, Sept 2009, with the title: "IN AT THE DEEP END. What happened when the World's Biggest Internet Pirates invaded one of the World's Biggest Art Exhibitions."

In 1855, the French artist Gustave Courbet submitted his now-famous painting *The Artist's Studio* to the World Exhibition in Paris. Although nobody realized it at the time, Courbet, the prophet of Realism, was making history by calling his painting "a real allegory". Instead of the old symbolic figures, he was painting people from real life – not just those writers, thinkers and poets that had influenced him (Proudhon, Baudelaire, Champfleury), but also priests, prostitutes and workers. All of those people portrayed were based on real, living characters, but also carefully chosen to tell a story – Courbet wanted his painting to display his thoughts about society at that time... what were the consequences of this new industrial society? And what could art's role be in it? The painting was refused. But, using his own money, Courbet rented a venue just next to the world fair, and displayed the painting anyway.

Fast-forward to 2009 and our Courbet-inspired "PadiglioneInternet" (The Internet Pavilion). It digs into a series of contemporaneous issues – threats of political restriction, the future of the internet, copyright, the art world itself; of borders, markets, curators, collectors, city marketing, and artists... the list goes on. It does so because of the fact that it is a virtual art pavilion, and as such the first of its kind at the Venice Biennale. All of this was clear to me when Miltos Manetas came up with the idea, and it has become more and more evident as the journey has unfolded.

It all began when Daniel Birnbaum offered us the chance to be an official part of the Venice Biennale, but to be there as an independent (although still part of the official structure – a "collateral project"). Miltos paid for this independence out of his own pocket. The Internet Pavilion therefore had a special position – in Venice, these collateral projects are the official sideshows, evaluated and accepted by the Venice Biennale, but not paid for. To be collateral denotes official status, and comes with a spread in the catalogue, and some promotion. Except for the Internet Pavilion, all the collateral projects are produced either by nations that do not have a national art pavilion of their own, or by large, official organizations.

The rest of the Biennale consists of course of the national pavilions, with their invited artists in the main curated exhibition (this year, under the theme of *Making Worlds*), all of which is organized on commission and under supervision from the board of directors. So, all artworks at the Biennale have gone through a series of evaluations to become an official part of the exhibition. That's how it works.

The Internet Pavilion is an outsider by definition – there has never been anything similar at the Venice Biennale before. The Padiglione Internet is a collateral project inside the Venice Biennale, but from the point of view of an independent artist, with an independent curator. Miltos (with me as sidekick) understood the possibility of being collateral – so, I asked my old friend Daniel Birnbaum if it was possible. He was very enthusiastic about the very idea. Miltos paid the fee – and, almost without knowing it, we were a collateral project and an official part of the Venice Biennale 2009. This gave us what we wanted – the opportunity to act in a different way. The internet points directly towards Gustave Courbet and art's strange relationship with the world beyond the art world, with "reality". And that reality is why the internet and art are not an easy match. The internet is fluid, changing, connecting, without borders and not at all tangible. I guess that is why there is so much at stake, globally, regarding the internet at the moment. The internet's existence is in opposition to a world that relies on industrial control. It is, quite simply, a new global reality, attracting millions and millions of users, and producing more statements per minute than anyone can handle.

The internet is all that the art world claims to be... or wishes it was. But the art world is, in reality, small. It is confined. The art world has not changed much since Courbet exhibited that painting in 1855. Its raison d'être is to produce salable, physical objects within a small industry of connoisseurs. But the art world is schizophrenic – it may be confined, but its marketing value is that it promotes ideas of "reality", "change", "freedom", "the new", "transformation"... People go to Venice to experience this "freedom" of art, and to get a glimpse of the reality from the point of view of the artists... but what is not so evident is that it is all launched from a confined art world and displayed within the walls of controlled exhibition spaces. The art world loves, in the tradition of Gustave Courbet, to embrace reality. In fact, the Venice Biennale could be seen as a huge "real allegory", with loads of artworks that claim to show the reality of today's society... but without Courbet's carefully planned scheme.

We decided to use the internet pavilion to let in this much talked-about reality, which is hard to avoid when dealing with the internet. Daniel Birnbaum understood that it would be difficult to introduce an internet pavilion that did not reflect the internet itself... but he had a tough time when the Pirate Bay's "Embassy Of Piracy" opened (a collaborative online art project created by the notorious Swedish peer-to-peer filesharing website, promoting freedom of the internet). The Biennale people wanted what they have always had, the one thing that has enabled them to maintain their brand – control. Rumor has it that they phoned from Rome on the morning that news of our pavilion went out. So, while we were talking with different stake-holders of the internet (commercial, non-commercial, pirates...) to see what their reaction was to the idea of an internet pavilion, we also remained a little vague to begin with, so we didn't get kicked out of the Biennale.

Essentially, PadiglioneInternet is a container rather than an exhibition – it is a platform. It's not propaganda in itself, but a host of different other entities, such as the Embassy Of Piracy. It collects different modes, attitudes and wishes that want to bring the art world together with the internet. It does all of this to create a platform for observations. In some ways, we acted as a Trojan horse for reality... for the reality of the internet, such as the Embassy Of Piracy. This way the internet pirates became part of the Venice Biennale. PadiglioneInternet acted as its own entity. There was no way of stopping them. And God knows, we never tried. PadiglioneInternet also made it clear that they themselves did not know where it would all end.

So, there was suddenly a project within the official structure of the Venice Biennale that nobody could control. Not us. Not the Biennale. Not even the pirates. Nobody.

The Embassy Of Piracy brought in the world, in a form of action and activism. It brought in a way of being that is based on collaboration instead of the "I" of the individual artist. Suddenly things became visible, tangible. The art world. The world of the internet. The world of politics.

PadigilioneInternet has its roots in a tiny, confined art world – but it made a connection to the real world. We invited in a virus, something uncontrollable – that energy around the Pirate Bay – just to see what would happen. We did also invite others but it was really only the pirates that responded. They wanted to go to Venice. Nobody else cared. Or were too scared. To me, PadiglioneInternet is not primarily about copyright issues. It is about the possibilities of a new world. But it is produced by people that understand marketing – and the issue of copyright is one that gets the attention. In the context of the Biennale, PadiglioneInternet was all about letting in a new reality – one that tells a different story about the future to an art world that is still stuck in 1855.

A couple of weeks later, the Pirate Bay temporarily renamed itself the Persian Bay – installing proxy-servers and many other elements designed to help the preservation of the internet and free communication in Iran – well, then it was obvious. The Embassy Of Piracy, the pirates, and a whole generation of internet users are "digging into" and even changing reality. For me, getting a glimpse of the "pirate generation" has been a learning experience – the world truly is changing and big things are at stake. We are at a crucial moment. The pirates are confronting it all, they are not letting reality down. They act. And they do so with a smile.

Therefore, PadiglioneInternet has only just begun. The other entities, the internet shows on this site, the AIDS-3D performance, the stuff that will be added during summer and up until the closing of the Venice Biennale, will all add to the story, forming a "real allegory" of today – Palle, Kristin and Tobias of the Pirate Bay... laughing; Daniel Birnbaum smiling, the board of directors behind him, worried; François Pinault (art collector) as the new Walt Disney of Venice; Joseph Brodsky; Jay Jopling in a taxi-boat; the people in Iran... and, in the middle, the artist, still alone, surrounded by a desert of blank computer screens and the sound of an ever-changing wind.

Jan Åman, July 12, 2009.

And here is some of my personal story related with the Internet Pavilion...

On March 20, I rented a car and started traveling all over America, searching for something different from what I already knew about the Internet.

Before starting this trip though, I spent a sleepless week in Paris. It was Paris Fashion Week and I was there because I had absolutely no idea from where else to start working towards the Internet Pavilion. Most people think that Fashion is a stupid occupation, probably because they never had the chance to live the somewhat shallow but definitely tragic beauty of the night during Paris fashion week.

This time though, the shows weren't that interesting. Maybe it was because of the recession but there wasn't anything really memorable except of a few moments at the Margiela's show which was also his final before moving out of his own business. At some point, I found myself alone at Le Montana's bathroom, thinking (between lines of exquisite cocaine) of the urgency to find a good architect who would design the Internet Pavilion.

Later that night, back at Le Marais, to the apartment of my very special and smart friend Benjamin Loyaute where I was staying. I woke him up asking him if he had any ideas.

«What about Tadao Ando» Benjamin said, «I can't really think any other architect than Ando at this hour. Maybe I can put you in touch with him, a friend of mine knows him well.»

The day after, I wrote to Mr. Ando.

Dear Mr. Ando,
What is "Internet" in terms of space? How do we walk in the Internet, how do we even circulate without dying from boredom? We want you to design the Internet Pavilion. We don't need any complicate Net-architecture, "Avatars", "Virtual Worlds" etc, that's actually what we want to avoid. We are interested instead for something poetic and influential, something suggestive such as the prints of Claude-Nicolas Ledoux.

But Tadao Ando was very busy and had no time to design the Internet Pavilion. So Jan Åman thought of Swedish architect Mia Hagg and her boyfriend at that time, the architect Jean Nouvel.

I called Mia and we agreed to meet at Le Fondation Cartier, where Nouvel was scheduled for a conversation with theorist Paul Virilio. The two were talking in French and for two hours, apart of a few words, I couldn't understand anything. So I sat back in my armchair and looking at them, I started writing the subtitles of what they were saying in my imagination. Soon, I felt as if I knew exactly what they were saying, particularly Virilio.

I haven't read any of Paul Virilio's books and I knew nothing about his ideas, yet his arguments, his obsessions and his paranoia, suddenly started parading around me, circulating me up to the point that I began feeling uncomfortable with my very own convictions. It was a very unusual thing, a kind of "psychoanalysis on speed", and as Virilio went on talking about the desert of the computer screens, I realized that I actually had a serious problem myself: that during the last ten years, I had become a victim of computers, a computer junkie!

In addition, my relationship to the Internet wasn't as glamorous as I had convinced myself and others. When finally the talk was over, I knew that the "internet" of the Internet Pavilion I was trying now to build, wasn't the kind of internet I really wanted.

```
«We need another Internet», I kept repeating to
myself a few days later, as I was flying to New
York. «This isn't "internet" enough, this is just
some kind of desert. The desert of computer screens
as Paul Virilio says.»
```

Arriving in NY, I went to visit the office of architect Christian Wassmann. I found him at his desk, playing with a little copy of Le Corbusier's Philips Pavilion.

The Philips Pavilion, whose floor plans are now lost, became an emblematic building especially for young architects.

Commissioned by Philips Electronics in 1956, the Pavilion wasn't supposed to display any commercial goods but showcase electronic technology in as many forms as possible. It had to serve the Arts and the improvement of humankind. Le Corbusier, who was enthusiastic about the idea, wrote: «I will not make a pavilion but an Electronic Poem and a vessel containing the poem; light, color image, rhythm and sound joined together in an organic synthesis.»

But as it happens, Le Corbusier was too busy to design the Philips Pavilion himself so his assistant, the Greek Architect and pioneer of Electronic music Iannis Xenakis, took over the design of the building and the final pavilion was a complex collaboration between Xenakis, Le Corbusier and the French composer, Edgard Varese.

The quest of Philips Pavilion, was that "Space has to meet Music" and even "become" music (under the spectrum of the new world of electronics).

So I asked Christian to come up with something like that.

```
«For the Internet Pavilion, we also want to turn
real space into internet. We want an Internet
Pavilion which is huge (in terms of space) and at
```

the same time extremely portable. Can you do it?»,
I asked.
«Well, I did something like that back on the days I
was a student.» Wassmann said.«I made a cube that
is a Litter which can be turned into a Meter. The
cube has the volume of a litter and weights a
kilogram. When you expand it, it becomes a meter.
It is made of a special translucent material and
when it's open, it looks like a bridge.»

In Los Angeles, I met with the Father of the Internet, Dr. Leonard Kleinrock.

I was told about Dr. Leonard Kleinrock for the very first time while in New York, explaining the Internet Pavilion to a friend.

«You should talk to Dr. Kleinrock about the
Internet Pavilion», my friend said. «I maybe able
to put you in touch with him actually, because his
daughter is a friend of mine.»

«Who is Mr. Kleinrock?», I asked my friend.
«You should know him, he is the inventor of the
Internet!»
«Isn't Tim Berners Lee who came with the World Wide
Web?»
«Yes but back in 1969, the year that we went to the
Moon, Mr. Kleinrock connected for the very first
time two university computers and sent the first
email from one computer to another.»

It was the year we landed to the Moon and only a very few people paid attention to Mr. Kleinrock's invention – the internet.

Look at the Moon, its as empty as ever, while Internet is now full of all kind of situations.

On April 27 – a Monday – I met Leonard Kleinrock at his UCLA laboratory. This is the same office, the 3420 Boelter Hall, where in September 1969, Dr. Kleinrock, turned his Host computer to the first node of the Internet. Finally, on 29 October 1969, he succeed sending the first message to a computer that was located 400 miles away, at the Stanford Research Institute.

«The text we tried sending» Mr. Kleinrock told me «was the command LOGIN. So we sent the 'L' and then we called Stanford on the telephone. "Did you receive the 'L'?" "Yes, we received the 'L'", Stanford replied. Then we sent the 'O' and we called them again. "Did you receive the 'O'?" "Yes, we did receive the 'O'", they answered. But when we tried to send the 'G' the system crashed. Hence, the literal first message that was sent over the Internet was 'LO' which is old English for the word 'Look'! Internet had arrived and it was asking all our attention!»

«Dr. Kleinrock, is it true that you are not happy with the Internet as it is today?», I asked him. «I read an interview of yours where you complain that with the existent Net, we can't connect from all places, we can't connect with all possible devices and also, that the devices that we are using to connect are still visible!»

«If I understand well, you want that internet exists everywhere, that we can connect with it with all possible objects and even that we will not have to use any device at all in order of connecting!»

«That's right», Mr. Kleinrock said, «internet is no good yet.»

«Am I wrong or you wish that internet becomes Nature? You don't need any devices to connect to Nature, its everywhere and you are always connected to it by all kind of objects.»

«Do you want that internet becomes just another layer of Nature?»

«Well, I never thought of it that way but yes, basically this is what I would like internet to be», said Mr. Kleinrock.

I left his office with that idea in mind. The only way to escape the desert of the computer screens, would be to create a new internet. That was the internet I wanted to show at my Internet Pavilion in Venice. But how this was possible? There was only a month left until the opening of the Biennial, where would I find such a network?

Finally, I went to Mountain Sinai...

Back to my studio in London, after that long American odyssey, I was exhausted.

During my trip, apart of Mr. Kleinrock, I had met a large number of hackers, activists, technologists. All of them, in one way or another, had enforced my desire for a new internet. I had also met Durek, a Haitian shaman based in Los Angeles, who also questioned my relationship with computers.

```
«'To screen' means 'to hide'», Durek told me. «When
you look stuff on screens, any kind of stuff, good
or bad, you simply get hypnotized. Screens exist to
hypnotize you, to make you think that everything is
OK.»
```

These words and Mr. Kleinrock's requests were in my mind as I was driving my car from San Francisco to Los Angeles, crossing a very green mountain area called Big Sur. So it was only at the very last moment, that I noticed a sign that was informing me that Henry Miller's Memorial Library was just a mile away. «A library dedicated to Henri Miller in the middle of the forest?», I wondered. It sounded "new internet" enough to me. So I stopped my car to its parking lot and went in to check the books. Immediately, a little volume hit my eye, it was a very peculiar edition of Homer's *Odyssey*.

I suddenly felt that some kind of...

(to be continued...)

www.manetas.com

http://cargocollective.com/manetas

www.superneen.com

www.padiglioneinternet.com